TRUTH,

My New Best Friend

NICOLE M. BENTLEY

Dr. Nes International Consulting & Publishing
P.O. Box 70167
Pasadena, CA 91117
www.drnesintl.com

Editor: Stefanie Manns
Editorial Proofer: Kia Stokes
Cover Design: Jessica Land

ISBN:9780999178591

DEDICATION

Martinae and Nyla, this serves as your guide. No matter what it looks like, always follow God's plan and Mommy's voice in you to help you along your way. Never ever feel defeated!
To the Love of my Life, Kevin, you are living proof that God's promises are really real. ❤ *Peace, Love &* TRUTH

ACKNOWLEGDEMENTS

This would not have even been possible without the encouragement of my Journey Sister Samantha Jefferson-Haynes, who prayed for me before, during and after the realization of my Naked Truth. She prayed me through the tough emotional days of my writing and celebrated my success along the way. That is a true sister/friend.

It is a must that I give praise and thanks to my absolutely amazing husband, Kevin J. Bentley. Baby you are the wind beneath my wings, I love you! You were as critical to this book getting done as I was. You allowed me to soar and you said you were proud to be my husband. These are the words that got me to the finish line!

Last but not least, to my beautiful mother Karla Robinson, you are an awesome mom and I'm proud to be your daughter. I could not have been blessed with a better mother, Mom I love you so much. I made it through!

~Nicole ♥

CONTENTS

NICOLE M. BENTLEY

Blank pages are intentional

PREFACE

I have accepted a lot of things in my lifetime. I mean, boy, these eyes and this heart have seen and experienced so much. Now don't get me wrong, I get that there is a price to be paid for the life that we are blessed to live. And often, that price is pain. So we endure circumstances and the challenges that come with life, whether they become our burdens by default or decision. We work that low-paying job to make ends meet. We struggle with the fallout of growing up without our fathers in our lives to give us that guiding hand, to help to make an imprint on our identity, and to be one of the firsts to teach us how special we are.

We accept our partner's infidelity and outside children, or the pain of losing a child, be it from a tragic incident or the unwavering choice of an abortion. We will accept and allow depression to set in and dismiss it as tiredness and just needing to sleep more.

We will accept the devastating pain of a friend betraying us and yet we continue to press forward. We will accept drastic weight gain and or loss and pass it off as if it's no big deal, when it could be attached to some serious heartache we are experiencing and we are trying to eat or starve the real problem away.

What we accept and allow in our lives is all our attempt to hide from the pain. And to avoid facing the TRUTH.

I am certain that you can see yourself in at least one of the situations that I've mentioned. I know that you've been allowing something, dealing with something, covering up and hiding something, running from something. All in an effort to not face what is really hurting you.

The one thing that most of us (yes, even you) may not be so easily and ready to accept is that many of the situations that we're in right now are a result of what we've allowed for far too long in our lives. The men that we've allowed to stay. The depression that we've allowed to stay. The hurt and pain that we've allowed to stay. All of it is running our lives because of the lies we've chosen to live. The truth that we've refused to face.

The denial ends today.

If I've struck a nerve and you are sick and tired of accepting everything that lands on your plate, then this book is for you. I am going to take you on a journey through my life, through my very own truth, in hopes that you will see yourself in it. I want you to see how you're not alone, never have been, and that the twists and turns of your life, the serious and emotional situations, that you've lived through were no coincidences. Not only will we walk through it all, but I want to offer you some insight as to why you've been in this consistent and very vicious cycle of pain, but you cannot find your way out. The solution, the prescription, to that pain is a combination of acceptance, self-love, and God. I will share with you how all three saved me—and helped me to see my truth.

This book is the first step to a new beginning—one in which you love yourself more fully and openly than you ever have before. Some people may argue that there is something wrong with doing that and someone who thinks only of themselves are very selfish or self-centered. Don't believe that lie. The way I look at it, if I'm not taking care of myself, mind, body, and soul, then nothing, and I do mean nothing, will operate properly around me. The same is true for you. So if you needed a permission slip to start loving yourself first, then here you are.

By the time this book comes to a close, you will have been on the craziest, happiest, funniest, and saddest emotional trip ever. As I unfold my life's story, I ask that you press into your own life, and examine where you are and where your heart wants to be. I pray you will walk away with a clear understanding of your value, love for yourself, and knowing that you can have exactly what God promises you, as long as you, hold on, and endure through to the end of your own process.

All of our journeys may have been different and our roadblocks have not been the same. But we've all had storms in our lives. We've all been through or are in, the process of pain. But for each of us, that pain is a teacher. When we accept that and understand exactly what God is seeking to teach us, we can move pass those storms that we encounter in life. As our best teacher, He is allowing us to find our way through, wind, rain, lighting, and all. He could easily point us to the way out right away, but as a good father, He wants us to learn these lessons on our own. That's how we learn best. So walk through those storms.

Think of this book as your raincoat with insight and inspiration to cover you. And allow your truth to be your light through the darkness. ❤ *Nicole Maria*

"Now faith is the substance of things hoped for, the evidence of things not seen."
Hebrews 11:1 KJV

INTRODUCTION

When life is good, it seems that nothing can go wrong. The things that have gone wrong in the past are long forgotten. We're happy and feeling on top of the world and full of joy.

Then we have those harder, more serious seasons when we are on the wrong track. We've taken one wrong turn after the next. Pain and heartbreak are coming from all angles. Life seems to be slamming us onto the pavement, mentally and, for some of us, physically.

Now during these times, some of us tend to be so sure that what we are going through and or dealing with is for sure someone else's fault. We tell ourselves things like:

"If I hadn't trusted what he said, and just left when that last thing happened…"

"If I had told his wife about us…"

"If I had decided not to keep the baby and to have the abortion…"

"I would not be dealing with this stress right now."

"My life would be good."

"I would be so much further in my life."

But none of those decisions that you made, probably in the name of love, were his fault. (We'll get into that later.) Nor did these choices stop anything that God has for you. (We'll talk about that too.) Where you are right now is a result of the truth about yourself that you chose to ignore. The who, what, why, and how you are. That's the answer to all. Acceptance. Feel it and face it. And when you do, like I did, you'll discover that is exactly where you are supposed to be.

I am going to encourage you to take it all the way back. Back to the little girl in the little apartment or house. The one who was innocent. The one who may have needed somebody who wasn't there. The one who learned nothing about love—for herself or otherwise. You'll take her hand and let her lead you on this truth journey. Trust me, she knows how to show you the way.

Being able to understand how your life began to change for the best or for the worse one thing is definitely necessary. You have to see where it all began and how your life unfolded from there. You have to see where you've been and what you've chosen to do. You must acknowledge your part in your life's twist and turns.

On my journey, I figured out along the way that everything that feels good doesn't mean that it is for your good. These are the times when we have to learn to press in and tighten up our intuition light bulbs, so we are sure we are seeing things in the brightest way possible, and realizing what this current life's track really is all about. Until you do that, you never know what is waiting for you to do.

For me, one of the things that was waiting on my life track was to tell my story. I never, ever thought I would write a book, but in recent years, I'd really started to unpack my life for what I hoped would be the last time. I started searching myself deeply, going back-and-forth about how I was loving and hating myself, emotionally, morally, and even physically. Then it finally dawned on me that those thoughts were beginning to force me to take a look at my own life's journey and where I had been. It was time for me to take a full look at my own life's process. When I did, I found so many answers to so many questions about myself, some of which I didn't know I had.

One of my biggest revelations on my journey was there were so many things I wish I had known. I wish someone could have openly shared their pain with me. I wish someone would have told me their truth. My, oh my, how I could have interrupted some of my heartache or mistakes. That's when I decided that I had to share my truth with as many women as I could.

After taking the time out for some self-reflection and looking at my own life joys, achievements, struggles and even disappointments, I realized there must be more women, like me, who struggled with pain. I couldn't have been the only one who'd spent so many sleepless nights alone, with only her thoughts and her tears to soothe her soul. So I decided (well honestly, God decided for me) that it was time for me to reveal my heart, my painful shame, and all of its ugly truth to go along with it.

Writing this book was to set myself free to live the life I was truly created for. I could take the mask off, and stop hiding in those shameful and dark shadows of my life. I could also offer others a light, like a lamp under their feet, to find their way. As I wrote and wrote, I began to clearly see there must be something in me that has been lying dormant. The energy is ready to be released. The new life is ready to be born.

While reflecting on some very painful and heart-wrenching memories, I understood those situations were always supposed to happen. Now I've come full circle, I can see the lessons in each one. I can see the healing that needed to take place. The heart that needed to be broken so it could come back together—stronger, open, and grateful. Had I not lived the life I did, I wouldn't be able to appreciate the life I have now. I am surrounded by love, peace, and truth. I am an authentic me that I am willing to allow everyone to see. No more darkness. No more secrets and lies. No more running from the truth.

Discovering my truth made me realize a lot of things. Let me share a few of them:

1. *We can't always blame others for our heartache and misfortune. We must, at some point, take full responsibility for the turns our lives have made.*

2. *We must be willing to accept the truth about what has happened, press into that truth, and pick ourselves up from there.*

3. *You will never be happy until you let go of where you've been so you can stand in where you are.*

When I learned to live by those words for myself, and find the good even in my heartache, that was the day I knew I would be able to live with my very own Naked Truth and release myself of the shame I had been hiding for way too long.

Allowing yourself to give in to your Naked Truth will breathe new energy, new life, into you. That energy becomes the strength to stop hiding behind your shame or allow others to harm you with the ugliness of the mistakes you may have made in your life. Once you have accepted your truth, no one can fight or condemn you with it. It's no longer a weapon to hurt you. You embrace it now. You accept it and embrace all of who you are. You start living again. As they say, your truth shall set you free.

I'm not telling you what I think. I'm telling you what I know to be the ABSOLUTE TRUTH. The day I let my truth guide me was the day the real Nicole was able to come out into the marvelous light. At last. That was day that I discovered my purpose and worth in life…

It was the start of the greatest journey I never knew I would be blessed to have.

1
LETTER TO MY FIRST LOVES

Being cheated out of having a father in her life is the first heartbreak a girl will ever have. Fathers are who give girls their identity in this world, the man who teaches her who she is. He shows her the way she should be treated, the way she should be spoken to, and the way she should be loved. Without a father, a girl never truly knows who she should be and who she should allow to access her heart. There is a piece of her that is always missing—a piece that she will never stop searching for. As you journey from a young adult to a woman, there is always this little ache that comes from all of the unanswered questions. That is when, for the first time, you're coming face-to-face with yourself, and the woman who you are versus the woman you know you want to be.

You may not see yourself in the best light. You may not feel pretty enough. You're wondering why you've dealt with the cheating, the lying, and the disrespect in your relationships, and why you've been treated the way you have by men who you thought loved you. Trying to make sense of why you've always been seeking, always searching to find that true love.

You never even considered that all this heartache stems from the lack of your father's presence in your life. The love and the emotional safety that you've been searching for is what you thought love was supposed to look like. It's the love you have for yourself, the love you could have only learned from him. But that love never showed up like you thought it would. Just like Daddy never did. And it takes a while for us to figure that out.

Discovering those answers would be easier if we had someone to piece it all together for us, to fill in the blanks so we could finally find the answers we needed. Or if we could go back and tell ourselves the truth about what was to come so that it wouldn't hit us so hard.

If I could go back and tell myself a thing or two it would go a little like this...

Good Morning and Happy 15th Birthday, Little Nikki!

Now I know you may not be feeling well and that morning sickness from that little bundle of joy inside of your belly may be giving you a fit. But you gotta get up and get ready for school. Today may not be a good day, but remember you are the one who chose to keep your baby and not go through with the abortion, even after your second visit to the clinic. So put a smile on your face. After all, it's your birthday! Soon enough you will give birth to a beautiful baby girl.

I hate to tell you this, but I have to. You may want to prepare now to do this on your own. He will not be around to help you raise her. Now don't get me wrong, after your mother puts you out again and you go live with your baby daddy and his family, you are going to be okay at first. You'll be settled and feel safe and believe that everything, from that point on, will be okay. And it will be until that morning when he jumps on you and fractures your jaw, while yanking your baby girl from your arms because you questioned where he was all night and why he didn't come home. I know it sounds scary but don't worry. After the police were called and you were transported to the hospital, your best friend's sister comes to pick you up. She took you back to your baby's dad's house to get your belongings and you'll get to live with your friend and her family for a while. Good news, right?

During this time you'll be really happy and things will be going great. The baby will be growing up and school will be pretty good. But after a while, you are going to find yourself feeling really sad, and you're not going to understand why. You will start going to see a counselor for a while to help with your sadness. It helps you and eventually you move back home with your mother where things are going amazing. You will run for Junior Queen at your high school and actually win! You are going to look so beautiful when they crown you. You will make it to your senior year and that's when things get tough again. Your high school counselor explains that somewhere along the lines he miscalculated your graduating credits after you returned back to school from when

19

your mother sent you to live with your father in Texas. Your counselor will try to explain that the school in Texas was on a different grading system and you're not going to have enough required credits to graduate and that you will have to come back the following year.

Now before you get mad about this, just know everything will be okay. You'll walk that stage because of God's grace and refusing to give up. It will be a beautiful day for you. A beautiful start to a new chapter in your life. Or so you thought...

Little Nikki, I want you to hear me out. After graduation, a lot happens. I'm not going to sugar coat it, Baby Girl. You are gonna go through hell and back again. You are going to feel so empty and unwanted that you're going to try to kill yourself. A serious bout with depression will haunt you because you will feel you are out here in the world with no mother to support you and no father in sight, no one to help you navigate your way through. You will make some bad decisions about men. You will be in an abusive relationship, you will be in several adulteress relationships with married men. You will go through with an abortion. Your life is going to have some ups and downs and some of your downs are gonna seem unbearable, but, just trust me, you will make it though.

As you transition into adulthood, you will always feel that someone is watching over you for some reason, and as you grow up you will come to understand why. I just want you to know that your lonely feelings will only be temporary and your lack of love will be over sooner than you think. You will come to understand that your choices in men were because you never had a good example from your father and you were just searching. Just know you will come into your own and a day will come when you will understand that you deserve so much more. You'll eventually see that just because you didn't have an example of love from your father, it doesn't mean you'll never find love. Trust and know your Father in heaven has covered you and He loves you so much. After you go through your heartbreaks, He will restore you and your heart. He will take those shattered pieces and piece them all back together. Your heart will be better than new.

So, Little Nikki, hold on. You are stronger than you know. What will seem like forever is only a short time. Be blessed and have faith. I'll Love You so much more later just wait! I will see you real soon!

Forever Together,
Big Nikki

You see, being able to understand my life now, everything that has happened to me makes sense. I've accepted that the father of my little-girl dreams does not exist. He was only in my imagination, an idea of what I thought I had. But the man who was actually a part of me wasn't anything like that. He wasn't there. My father was a selfish, angry drunk, and a man that doesn't take credit for his mistakes or take care of ALL of his responsibilities.

I am writing these words for the child in me, first, and not really for anyone else. Today, I am burying the broken- hearted little girl that always waited for Daddy to come and he never ever did. To completely close this wound, I have some words for him too.

Daddy,

Wherever you are, you cheated me out of knowing and understanding what real unconditional love was from a man. You allowed me to go out into the world looking for that love from other men and in relationships that constantly broke my heart just like you did. I'm so thankful that I found out who God the Father was. He became for me what I thought I could only get from you. God is who I had to talk to when things got rough or when my heart was being abused and broken. My God never, ever left me, and I could call on him even when I was wrong and He loved me in spite of my mistakes.

The truth is there was one thing you were consistent with, and that was making everything about you. The few times that I saw you and tried to ask you why you didn't love me, you always reminded me that you were "the father who helped make me." And you know what, Daddy? You are right. You did help me to become who I am, just not in the way you want to believe. Since you were not in my life, I became an amazing woman, awesome mother, and now wife. I'm not mad at you at all, wherever you are. Had it not been for you, I would not be who I am. I would not have fought as hard as I did for the life I have.

So I hope the decisions you've made about choosing not to be a father to me sit well with you. My decision about letting you go sits well with me. I am letting all of it go. Including you. ~Nikki

Blessed are the fatherless daughters who forgive their fathers for never being there!

"I know the thoughts that I think towards you, saith the Lord, thoughts of peace, and not of evil, to give you an expected end, Then Shall ye call upon me, and ye shall go and pray unto me, and I will hearken unto you. And ye shall search for me with all your heart"
Jeremiah 29:11-13 KJV

NICOLE M. BENTLEY

spanked as a small child. Ever. Maybe that's what was wrong with me. I needed more butt whoppin's.

One time, my mother's boyfriend gave me a spanking for lying. He had every right to punish me since he was really like my dad. He and my mother had been together since I was about two years old and until I was eleven or twelve. He was really a nice man. He stepped right in and did all the things a girl imagined her father would. He told me he loved me and showed me in his actions too. He bought me things, took me places, and always told me to act like a lady no matter where I was going. He was the person that taught and showed me what fine dining and quality shopping was. He taught me dining etiquette, how to speak properly, how to sit, and even how to eat a balanced diet. He really stressed eating my vegetables and he also taught me what being a classy lady was supposed to look and behave like. Because of him, I was the perfect young lady.

He was an amazing tailor and made a lot of my clothing during the time he was with my mother. They used to dress me like a little baby doll. (No I'm really serious.) In my beautiful dresses and matching hats, shoes, and tights, I looked like they took me right off of the shelf. Those were some really happy times in my life. That's when I felt the most loved.

But like most kids, when he tried to discipline me, all of that went out of the window. When he spanked me that time, I pulled the classic you're-not-my-daddy card that every stepchild is famous for whenever things don't go their way. I remember getting really mad and calling my dad to tell him what happened.

Now, you see, that phone call to my biological father was out of pure anger just because I didn't want to be spanked. But hey who does? Boy did I tick my mom off big time. When she got home from work, she beat my butt. And I deserved it.

My real father had nothing to do with my day-to-day and didn't do anything to support me. He lived in Texas and had not been there since I was born. His appearances were as rare as falling stars—you know you only see them every now and then.

Aside from not seeing him often, what I remember most about my dad was how he looked. My father was a pretty flashy kind of man—wild suits, open shirts, leather jackets. You know, someone who looked like he was in Prince's band and in town on the Purple Rain tour.

I remember one Christmas holiday when I was about seven years old, my father and his brother, who also lived in Texas, came into town. It was really cold outside, and when they arrived it was night time. It was pretty normal that I would spend the night with my grandmother if my father was coming into town, and she let me stay up late that night to wait for him.

Whenever he came to see me, he never stayed for a long time. It seemed like he was just there for a few minutes, long enough to ask me all of the questions that a good father should ask, like how I liked school and did I have any friends. That night was no different. A hug and a kiss, a few questions, and he was gone. Just like always.

I don't have many loving or memorable moments with my father because he was simply not there enough. There was a part of me that always tried to convince myself that I could count on him, and if I called him he would be there. And there was one time in my entire life when he was.

When I was 15, I found myself getting in the car with him and everything I owned. My mother found out I was pregnant and insisted I get an abortion. We fought about it for weeks, and I'd gone to the clinic twice to have the procedure, but backed out each time.

On the second visit to the clinic, my grandmother pulled up to the front of our house, with my mother in the front seat of the car and me in the back. I knew my mother was furious, and I had sense enough to not say a word. My mother got out of the car, slammed the door, and stormed in the house. Knowing I could not sit in the car forever, I opened the door slowly. I was scared and confused about what would happen next, but I knew for sure that I didn't want the abortion. Before I could get out of the car, my grandmother stopped me.

"Nikki, baby, if you want your baby, you keep your baby. I'm still gonna love you no matter what."

"I love you too, Granny," I responded. I was so relieved that I still had someone who loved me.

I came in the house cautiously, unsure of what my mom would say or do. One look in her eyes, I knew that she was still as angry as I thought. "If you are going to have that baby, you won't have it living in this house," she said as she called my dad. She called him to come get me.

Within a few days, I was shipped off to Atlanta, Texas to live with a man I didn't know and who clearly knew nothing about me. I was set to move in with him, his wife, and my two half-brothers. The plan was for me to go to school and to raise my child there.

I began my sophomore year of high school at small, country Atlanta High School, in Texarkana, Texas. I hated every minute of it. I didn't know anyone and I was much older than my brothers so they didn't go to school with me. My Dad drove me to school each day because he didn't want me riding the school bus pregnant. He didn't think it was safe.

Just imagine, here I am at this school where no one knows me. As the new girl, I stand out in every way. It's clear by the way I talk and dress in the latest clothes and shoes that I am different from everyone else. On top of that, I had a noticeably big belly with a baby inside of it. I was that girl, the one who everyone knew was having sex for sure. I hated it. The school, my dad's house, everything. I was a long way from St. Louis. And I felt it.

One evening I was on the phone talking to my grandmother. It was around the holidays and she was telling me they were coming down for Christmas to visit. I was excited at the idea of seeing her and the rest of my family, but that feeling was short lived. I got so upset thinking about how much I missed home. It all came out.

"I hate it here," I told her.

I was emotional, but I was also being honest. Living with my dad was horrible. I went on to say he didn't know me and he don't even know how to be my Dad and I was pregnant. I explained to her I wanted to come back home and I would go live with my aunt, my mom's eldest sister. She'd already told me I could move with her. I was going on and on, just as my father walked in.

He started yelling at me, telling me to not call his mother about not wanting to be there because I was staying there.

"Your mother put you out and I am responsible for you!"

We started arguing and throwing angry words back and forth at each other. I don't remember everything that was said, but there were some words that came out of my mouth before I had a chance to think. Words that took our argument to a new level.

"You ain't none of my daddy."

Right then he raised his hand and slapped me in my face while I held the phone and my grandmother yelled my name on the other end. I screamed and cried, trying to tell my grandmother what had just happened through my tears. She told me to calm down and that she would see me in a couple of days for the Christmas holiday.

"Put your father on the phone," she said.

I did what she told me to do, and sat there with my head down, still heated and shocked, while she spoke to him. When my father hung up the phone, he tried to apologize for hitting me. I just sat there so hurt and emotional from what had just happened. On top of everything else, being pregnant meant that my hormones were already all over the place. I could not accept anything he had to say. I had to go.

Needless to say, Christmas came and went and I was back in St. Louis living with my aunt before the new year. I got re-enrolled in my old high school and finished out the remainder of my sophomore year. I was set to be a junior after I had my baby, but I was devastated to find out that the school I attended in Texas and my current one were not on the same grading scale. So after my beautiful baby girl was born in May of that year, I began what would have been my junior year as a reclassified sophomore. I knew that I had to figure something out. I could not lose a whole year.

I went to my guidance counselor in hopes that I could plead a strong enough case to him to convince the school to change their mind. I was lucky—he was on my side and came up with a plan for me to still be able to graduate with my class. It wouldn't be easy; in addition to my regular class schedule, I would have to take six night school classes, and I couldn't fail any of them. If I didn't pass all of my classes that year or the following year, I wouldn't graduate. No second chances.

And the academic requirements were just one half of my battle. The other was paying for these classes. I soon learned that, for students who have fallen behind, the board of education only paid for two evening classes per year to get back on track. Anything beyond that was for the student to figure out on their own. Your choice was pay out of pocket for any extra classes needed or return to school until the requirements had been satisfied.

I had no clue how I was going to make this work. Here I am, a seventeen-year-old mother with a brand-new baby at home who needed my care and the stress of taking all of my normal classes plus some. I could have easily cried and given up. I can't lie, there were some tears. There were some doubts. This wasn't fair. I should have had parents and people to support me, financially and otherwise, so I wouldn't have to figure all of this out on my own. But in between all of those tears and thoughts, I came to a fast conclusion that the situation wasn't going anywhere. I had to deal with what I'd been dealt. I had to prove to myself, my daughter, my family, and even the people at school who doubted me that my decision to have a baby wasn't going to stop my life.

Hey, when you make grown up decisions you have to handle business like a grown up, I told myself.

It was hard, a lot of lost sleep and sacrifice, but, a few months later, I was almost at the finish line. It was what is known in high schools everywhere as "Senior Week," those last few days of school after prom leading up to graduation. Aside from the actual graduation ceremony, the highlight of that week is picking up your cap and gown. That's what makes it real. And for most students, by this point, there should be no reason to worry. If you weren't graduating for some reason, you would have known it by now. I didn't think I had anything to be concerned about. I was super geeked and ready to walk that stage with my class to prove to those who said I was making a mistake in keeping my baby—that I did it on my own and my hard work and dedication has paid off. My baby girl could be proud of me for hanging in there, being responsible, and completing high school on time even with the obstacles in my way. I couldn't wait to get that diploma in my hands.

Smiling from ear to ear, I walked into the guidance counselor office to turn in my senior card, an informal record signed by all of my teachers, who had signed to prove I would be passing all classes for the end of the school year and I had satisfied the credit requirements. As I walked to my counselor's desk to hand him my card, he asked me to have a seat so he could take a look at my transcript. While he was going over my stuff, I laughed and joked with my other classmates that were in the office; we were all so hyped. We were in the guidance office turned all the way up, yelling and chanting, "Summmmmmner '96, Summmmmmner '96!" You couldn't tell any of us anything. It felt good knowing that all of the underclassman were watching and hating on us. This was our time, our moment to shine. This was going to be our summer.

My counselor called my name to get my attention. I stepped up to the desk, waiting for him to hand me my card back so I could get in line with everyone else to get my cap and gown. "Nicole, I am sorry and I don't understand what happened. But looking over your transcript again, you are ½ of a credit short and you will not be able to graduate. You will have to either go to summer school and get your diploma later this summer or come back to school next school year and finish. You will get your diploma once the requirement credit has been completed."

At that moment, I felt like everything around me started moving in slow motion. I couldn't hear my classmates laughing or even what the counselor was saying. I was enraged and all I saw was red.

I stood up at his desk and began to yell as tears began to fall from my eyes.

"What do you mean I don't have enough? I can't be here next year! I have a daughter! You don't understand. I don't have any help with her I have to get a job.

No this isn't right. I did everything you told me. We went over everything. How could you let this happen?"

That was the Rated PG version, ya'll. I was so emotionally distraught, I didn't realize that I'd been cursing and lunging at the man. Things got so heated that the advising senior counselor, Mrs. Cavitt, came over and ordered me to the principal's office for my foul language and the outburst I displayed in the office. Crying uncontrollably as I walked down the hall, the secretary told me to have a seat. She said the principal was in a meeting and he would call me back shortly. As I sat there with no idea of what my next step for my life was, all I could think of was my baby and how I felt all my hard work was for nothing. I was so disappointed in myself for allowing all this to happen. I know I was raised to be a lady and respectful and I just lost it.

I sat there for what felt like hours until he called me into the office.

"Nicole, am I hearing this correctly, you were about to attack your guidance counselor?" With a genuinely concerned look on his face, he spoke calmly while handing me a Kleenex to wipe my face and nose that were covered in tears and running with snot.

I looked up at him as I wiped my eyes. "Sir, I wasn't going to hit him, but you have to understand why I am so very upset." He sat on the edge of his desk while looking at me sitting there in the chair in front of him. "I'm listening."

I went on to explain everything. "Sir, that's just not right. I did everything I was supposed to do—"

He put his hand up and stopped me mid-sentence. "Nicole, you can't take that many night school classes my dear, you only get two."

"I know. I paid for the other ones and the books that were needed. Why should I be punished because he messed up my transcript? I can't be here next year. I have a baby and she has to see me walk that graduation stage with my class. I have to get a job to support her. I just can't be here!"

He looked at me with sincere eyes as I wiped the tears that

were continuously falling down my face "Nicole, although this is horrible, the truth still remains. If you don't have the requirements, you can't graduate. And you are not allowed to participate in the commencement ceremony if you are not graduating with all that is needed. It is against policy." He went on to say they have allowed students to do that in the past and they never came back to satisfy their requirements.

When he told me that, I felt like maybe all hope wasn't lost. "I promise, whatever I have to do I will do. I have to walk for my baby, I just have to. My mother was a 15-year-old mother, my father's mother was a 15-year-old mother, and I was also pregnant at 15. So, see, I need this so I can begin to break this curse on my family. I need my daughter to see me achieve this."

"Stand up," he instructed. He stood from the desk and placed his hands on my shoulder, while looking me in the eyes. "I could lose my job for this, but I am going to call the guidance office and advise that everything has been worked out and they are to issue you your ceremony cap and gown. And, young lady, I need you to hear me. After the ceremony, all graduating students will report to the cafeteria to pick up the envelope with their diploma, you will not respond because you won't have one. You have to promise me you will respond to summer school and receive the remainder of your requirements to receive your diploma."

I wrapped my arms around him so strong and tight and cried so hard. A quivering, "YES SIR!" was all I could get out at first. I kept promising him over and over that I would keep my word and thanking him so much for allowing me to do this.

"Nicole," he stopped me as I turned to walk out. "This stays between you and me."

I looked back with the biggest smile imaginable.
"Yes, SIR!"

There are no words that can express the level of gratitude and sense of accomplishment I had waking up on the morning of June 6, 1996. As I got dressed and placing that ceremonial gown and cap on, I know I didn't stop smiling. Not once. Getting my baby girl ready and seeing her innocent, smiling face made it all worth it. She had no idea what she was about to witness or what this moment meant for her or me.

As my graduating class and I marched into the auditorium to the sounds of the Mighty Sumner Bulldogs drumline playing the renowned "Dogs Get Ready To Roll," our school song, my heart was beating along with the powerful sound of those drums. This overwhelming feeling of God's favor fell over me, and although I knew I would not receive my official diploma that day, at that moment it didn't matter. Paper or no paper, right then, I knew moving forward there would be nothing I would not try to accomplish. I had a daughter that would be watching my every move and I always wanted her to be proud of me and be honored to call me her mom.

That part of my life taught me there will be times when we make decisions, not thinking about what or how it will affect us later down the line. But, regardless of what choices we make, we have to stand on those decisions and never have regrets. Be it a bad decision or good decision, it has purpose, and that is for us to grow, stretch, and learn from our life's experiences.

The Naked Truth

You may have to walk through situations alone or you may have someone like my high school principal to help you along the way. The person is like an angel that God has allowed to come along and help show you some grace and mercy, but what you have to know is that you will get through it. You will get to the other side. Never, ever give up on yourself and always strive to be better. Set out to complete what you start. You never know what angels may be waiting on you to help get you to that next phase. But no one can do their part to support you if you never show up to do yours.

And know this too—the life that you have is the life you are supposed to have, no matter the struggles. God built you to withstand these blows. He gave you the strength to struggle and to make it through that fire. He knew that you would overcome those obstacles and make a way out of no way. It doesn't matter if you have the mom or the dad or the friends to love you in the midst of it all. You will get your blessings regardless. You will make it.

Just know your greater is coming. Just hold on and trust that what you need is already down on the inside of you.

You have strength. You have fight. You have heart. Use all of that.

"If what has been built survives, the builder will receive a reward."
1 Corinthians 3:14 NIV

NICOLE M. BENTLEY

3

BEHIND CLOSE DOORS

I am laying in this bed at my friend's house, feeling so sad and displaced. Everything in my life feels so out of control. I don't know what's going to happen from day-to-day. Will I have somewhere for me and my baby to stay? Can I take care of us? Did anybody want me? Do I even want to live?

I didn't know that it was possible to feel that alone. But I do. My mother didn't want me. We were not getting along at all. She never forgave me for getting pregnant, and I don't think she ever will. But how was I supposed to know what would happen? She never talked to me about sex and not getting pregnant. Yeah, she put me on the pill, but she didn't say anything else about not missing a dose or trying to take it at the same time every day. My father wasn't around to talk to me about boys and giving my heart and body away and what to demand from a man before I did. I just didn't know. And now, it was too late.

Here I was with a damn baby. What am I supposed to be doing,

I can't even support my doggone self. My baby's father was a bum out in these streets, doing what he wanted and not doing jack for our daughter. Heck, he even had another baby the same age as ours.

The demon of depression was on me, and I didn't know what to do with all of the thoughts racing through my head.

Dang, I feel like a fool.

You know what, maybe while my baby is over at her father's house with his mother (because I'm sure he's running the street) maybe I should just leave all of this.

I'll be better off just not even being around. Maybe, just maybe, if I wasn't here, I won't even have to worry about any of this anymore. I wouldn't have to think about where I would live, how I would take care of my daughter, not feeling wanted, or what I look like on some damn welfare. I feel like a straight ghetto girl, I was not raised like this.

I stared at the ceiling and the four walls, feeling trapped. I could hear my friend's sister getting ready to go to work. I wanted to get up to pee, but I knew I wouldn't be able to avoid her if I went to the bathroom. I just needed her to leave. I didn't feel like having the same conversation over and over again. She would ask, "What's wrong with you? Why you looking like that?" I would lie like I always do and say, "I'm fine, I just woke up. I'm tired," as I open the door to the bedroom and try to rush into the bathroom before she could say anything else. I knew I looked as bad as I felt inside. I couldn't hide it anymore. I stopped trying.

Just as I thought, I come out of the room, and just as I turn the corner to push the bathroom door open, here she goes coming up the steps.
"Good morning, Nikki. Hey, are you good today?"

"I'm fine," I mumble as low as I can.

"No, you're not. What's wrong?"

"I said, I'm fine!" I closed the bathroom door while she stood there, still talking. She always asking me something, shoot. Leave me alone. If you see I'm in a mood why you talkin' to me? I thought to myself as I closed the door to use the toilet.

I knew it was obvious that I was going through something. I looked at myself in the mirror as I washed my hands.
I am looking so raggedy.

My life got to be horrible that I didn't even feel like taking a shower in the morning. I couldn't shake this feeling of sadness that had come over me. But I knew I couldn't go on like this. You know what? This has to stop. Today is it. I gave myself a pep talk in the mirror. I had to get myself together.

My friend's sister yelled from the other side of the door.

"Nikki, I'm leaving for work."

"Oh, okay."

"You going to be okay?"

I assured her I would be good.

"Alright I'll see you later. My mom won't be home until super late, she has a singing set tonight at the club in Illinois but it's some leftovers in the refrigerator if you get hungry later. Is the baby coming home tonight?

"No she's staying out there with her daddy."

"Okay, well I'll see you when I get off work tonight."

I heard the front door close a few minutes later. Good, I can finally be alone.

In my mind, I was going to get something to eat and take a shower. But my body said something different. Back to the bed I went.
The simple things, like looking at the sun, made me sad. I don't even want to face the day. Not having my baby with me didn't

help. She was my distraction from how down I had started to feel. Without her, I was just alone with all of my sadness and confusion.

I drifted off for what I thought was a short nap. I blinked a few times and sat up to clear my head and remember where I was. The clock read 8 o'clock. What I thought was dozing off for an hour or so turned into sleeping the whole day away. Ya girl had been out for five hours.

Somewhat panicked, I put my feet on the floor with every intention to move. I didn't want anyone to come home and find me in the same old, funky t-shirt, pajama bottoms, and unwashed face from this morning.

I guess I'll get my butt up, shower and throw some fresh clothes on and try to eat me something.

I guess my stomach and brain finally connected and realized I hadn't had anything to eat all day. Deciding that food was the first on my to-do list, I headed to the kitchen and pulled some leftovers from the fridge. As soon as I lifted the fork to my mouth for the first bite, my phone rang.

"Hello?" Knowing it was my daughter's father on the other end, I answered with all of the attitude he deserved.
"Hey, what's up?"

"What's up?" I repeated his words back to him, with extra sauce. How dare he ask me such a stupid question?

"What's wrong with you?"

I chose not to go down the long road that I could have.
"Nothing. What's up?"

"My momma wanted to know if you wanted her to wash our daughter's clothes before I brought her back to you tomorrow?"

"That's fine, she can." I held the phone in silence, doing everything I could to keep my cool.

"Oh, and I'm not going to be able to give that money to you when I drop her off, something came up and I couldn't get it all."

"WHAT?!?!" I lost it. "See that's what I'm talking about. Can't depend on you for jack! So what am I supposed to do about her daycare fees?"

He was unfazed by how heated I was. "Like I said, I ain't got it."

"Yeah a'ight. Whatever!"

I slammed the phone down. "I am so sick and tired of the same damn thing!" I screamed to the top of my lungs to an empty kitchen. "Every time I need something he don't have it. It's always something with his broke ass. I'm so sick of doing this by myself.

I'm sick of crying about it, I'm sick of being so damn needy and feeling so alone."

I could do nothing but cry. I loved my baby, I loved her so much, but in that moment, I felt defeated. I didn't think I could give her what she needed. Love had nothing to do with putting food in her mouth, clothes on her back, and a roof over her head. I couldn't even afford to send her to daycare while I went to work, if I had a job. It was all too much.

I walked up the steps to the bathroom, and opened the medicine cabinet. I started grabbing all of the pill bottles I saw that were full, and, without even thinking, I opened them one by one, poured handfuls of capsules in my hand and started swallowing them. I drank some water out of the faucet to choke them down, tossed the empty bottle in the sink, and picked up the next one. Pour pills, swallow, water, pour more pills, swallow again.

My tears started to blind me, and those that my eyes couldn't hold spilled over onto my face. I slid down to the floor, my shirt soaked from faucet water and me crying so uncontrollably hard. I just need the pain and sadness to stop. I just didn't care anymore.

As I sat there on the bathroom floor sobbing, I felt like I just needed to get out of there. I vaguely remember leaving the house and walking towards the interstate. Wobbling was more like it. The effects of all of the drugs that I'd shoved down my throat were starting to take effect. I started to feel funny, lightheaded. I felt myself staggering down the concrete walkway, and next thing I know, I was on the overpass of the interstate. Everything went black.

I hear someone screaming my name. They sound hysterical and so far away. My eyes felt so heavy, but something in me told me to open them. I saw my friend's sister standing over me, crying.

"Nikki wake up! What did you do? Nikki what did you do?"
I didn't know what was happening. I realized that I was in a hospital. I knew something bad happened, but everything after I blacked out was a complete blur.

When I came to, I found out that the doctors had to pump my stomach to get the prescription medicines I had taken out of my system. Apparently, the doctor told my friend's mom if they had not got me to the hospital when they did, I may not have made it. They found out that I tried to commit suicide.

I can clearly remember my friend's mother making two phone calls, one to my mom to let her know what happened (of course, she got no answer and no return call) and the second to my grandmother who had been recovering from breast cancer surgery. My grandmother told my friend's mom she could not come to see me, but she would definitely contact the church and have one of the pastors come to the hospital to pray and sit with me.

After I was stabilized in the ER, I was moved to an ICU room by myself. It was so quiet, which surprised me. I was used to chaos in hospitals, with nurses and doctors moving around all hours of the day and night. It turns out they placed me on that floor because there were no more beds in the psychiatric unit. The nurse came in and asked me if I wanted something to eat. I felt comatosed. I had this blank look on my face. I didn't speak. I wouldn't talk or watch television. I just stared and cried.

Reverend Reed, from my grandmother's church, came to the hospital that night. He told me that my grandmother had called, and that something was happening to her baby and she didn't know what. She asked him to please come and pray for me, so he did. He sat by my bedside, prayed over me, and read scripture. I couldn't fully appreciate it then, but it comforted me to have someone bring the spirit and protection of God into that room and over my life. I was so lost, but Reverend Reed reminded me that Jesus had not left my side, and He never would.

The next day, my mother contacted the hospital after she got off from work. It wasn't new to me that I wasn't important enough for her to come running to find out what was wrong with me right away. She let an entire day pass before even picking up the phone to find out if I was dead or alive.

I was lying in bed when she walked into my hospital room. She was rigid and obviously uncomfortable. She didn't run over to my bed with a concerned look on her face or tears in her eyes. Anyone looking at the two of us from a distance would have wondered if we were related, much less mother and daughter.

"Hey," she said without an ounce of love in her voice.

I stayed quiet and didn't look in her direction.

She sat in a chair near the window on the side of my bed. The air was so thick between us that I started to notice her fidget more and more. She eventually turned on the television and pretended to watch while I continued to stare at the ceiling as if she wasn't there. She never tried to start a conversation with me or ask how I was feeling. I was waiting for her to say something, anything. No, were weren't in a good place, but she was my mother. Nothing that would have happened between us would have mattered if she'd just used that moment to at least ask me what happened, or to say anything to let me know that she still cared about me. I just needed to feel some type of love from her, from anyone. But she refused. I'd never felt more lonely and scared in my life.

We sat there saying nothing for hours.

That evening, my friend's mom and sister came back to the room, this time, with my daughter. As my friend walked into the room holding her, I started to cry and waved frantically at them to leave. I couldn't let my baby see me like this.

"No, no, I don't want her in here, please! I don't want her in here." I just kept shaking my head from side to side, begging them not to come any further.

My friend looked so sad, but she understood. She turned to take the baby outside, but not before I peeked at my daughter's sweet, innocent face. She was wearing her cute little purple and gold Lakers sweat suit. She had no idea what was going on around her, and that her mommy was in trouble and had tried to take herself out of this world. I couldn't hold back my tears. I cried uncontrollably. She didn't deserve this. She should have someone better than me to take care of her.

I'd swallowed those pills, hoping that my life would have been over. I wouldn't have to ever see her face. I wouldn't be lying in the hospital bed, broken, confused, and overwhelmed with guilt from making a decision four years ago to keep her only to not be able to take care of her.

I felt so selfish. I kept her here and I was supposed to be able to give her everything she wanted and needed. I had just turned away from the only person in the world who I knew loved me unconditionally. I felt so ashamed and so stupid.

My friend's mom came in and hugged me so tight. "Nikki, it's going to be okay, baby. It's going to be okay. If you need to cry, cry baby. But tell us what's wrong."

I started to breakdown again. Just when I thought I had no more tears to cry, they just kept coming.

She kept holding me. "Tell us what's going on with you. Why would you want to hurt yourself like this? Don't you know that baby needs you and she loves you?"

I couldn't find any words. There was nothing to say. I didn't know what got me here. I just knew I didn't want to live a life this hard. I didn't want to disappoint my daughter. I didn't want to do anything, including breathe. I laid there in silence. My friend's mom tried to make polite conversation with my mother who was still there. I just listened to them try to make awkward small talk. I really just wanted everyone to leave. The nurses coming in and out of the room to check in on me were a welcomed distraction.

As it started to get late, everyone started to gather their things to leave. By this time, my baby girl was asleep, so my friend bought her back into to the room to say goodbye. I was too tired to protest, and, besides, I knew she probably wouldn't wake up until she got home. I gave her a quick kiss on the forehead. My friend's mom assured me they would see me soon. She also let me know that she'd left their contact information with the nurse in case I needed anything.

"And don't worry about the baby. I'll take care of her for however long you need me to."

I looked at her and didn't say anything. I know she saw the tears welling up in my eyes and I hoped she could read my mind. I was grateful to know that my baby girl was safe and being taken care of.

They headed out, and my mom told me that she was going to find a bathroom. She was gone for a few minutes, and came back into the room and over to my bed.

"I'll see you later." She leaned over and gave me an awkward kiss on the side of my head. I wouldn't see her again until after I was released from the hospital four days later.

The next day, the nurse came into the room swinging open my curtains and raising my shade.

"Now sweetheart, you've been in this hospital going on three days. If you don't start eating, we're going to give you a feeding tube. You have to eat something." She checked my pulse and other vitals as she spoke.

"The doctor is planning to move you out of ICU today and to another floor or release you. There's going to be a psychiatrist that's going to come in to talk to you this morning to give you an evaluation." She paused and looked at me, begging me with her eyes to say something. I didn't.

She sighed and kept straightening things around the room. "Nicole, you must look over the menu and choose something to eat. Anything. But you have to start eating." She patted my legs, sighed again, and left.

A few hours later I decided to try to eat. Even lying down, I felt a little woozy and nauseous, and I knew that meant I needed to eat something. I ordered lunch, but when the tray came, I only took a few bites of strawberry Jell-O. It sunk to the bottom of my stomach like a rock. I couldn't eat anymore.

As the nurse warned, the psychiatrist came to speak with me. She asked me a lot of questions, most of which I answered with one word. No more than three. She nodded, wrote, and kept probing me.

"Do you still want to die, Nicole?"

It was hard to believe that I was actually sitting there with someone I didn't know, calmly talking about ending my life as naturally as I would talk about the weather. I should have been afraid to tell the truth, but I wasn't.

"Yes," I said, practically whispering. The stream of tears came on like a faucet.

"It's better this way." I don't know why, but I felt the need to explain myself so she didn't think I just wanted to end my life for no reason. I'd thought about this for a long time, and I'd come to the conclusion that nothing could be worse than how I was feeling. My daughter would be better off with someone who could take care of her.

The psychiatrist listened and kept writing. Then she got up and left the room for a minute. I didn't know what she was going to say when she came back into the room.

"You are going to be moved to another room in a little while, and I will be back to see you tomorrow at some point to speak with you again.

Nicole, I would like to just say, you may not have much to say right now and I know you don't think I understand your pain. But you cry. Nicole, it is really okay to cry. I have hope that your tears will turn into words so I can help you get the pain on the inside of you out. I looked up at her, with a tiny bit of reassurance. She gave me an endearing smile.

"I will see you tomorrow, Nicole."

Later that afternoon, I was moved to the fourth floor of the hospital. As the orderly wheeled my hospital bed past the nurse's station, I saw large, white storks and pink and blue baby blankets that, from a distance, looked like they had baby names on them, painted on the walls. As we kept going down the hallway, there were empty, clear baby cribs lined up against the wall. I was on the maternity unit. My heart started to ache.

Looking at those cribs only reminded me of when I gave birth to my baby girl at this very same hospital, almost four years prior. After the aide pushed my bed up against the wall and locked it in place, I was surrounded by soft pink . All I could think was, How did I get to this place? Wanting to take my own life? Like seriously, Nicole, you are tripping. What are you thinking about? Do you really want to leave your baby, the baby you said that you would love and that would love you when no one else would? The same baby you went against your mother to keep after going to not one but two abortion appointments. The baby you got shipped away for because your mother would not have you in her home with a baby.

I began to sob uncontrollably, thinking about how close I came to dying! I could have been dead instead of lying in that hospital, sobbing about my daughter. My tears soaked the pillow.

I heard the door to my room open, and I looked over my shoulder to see my Great Aunt Gloria standing there. I wiped my face and sat up, smiling to myself as I looked down and saw that she was carrying the one thing she never went anywhere without—her favorite black leather purse with the brass double-ball latch that closed it at the very top. Her purse was hanging from her forearm, and she clutched her blue Bible case to the center of her bosom. She looked at me with the most angelic and peaceful smile on her face.

"Nikki, sweetheart, how is auntie's baby?" She closed my door behind her and began to walk to my bedside. I sat up, and before I could even say one word, she sat her purse and Bible down on the foot of my bed. With her soft, yet aged, wrinkled hands, she grabbed me and pulled me to her chest. She held me in her arms and started to pray.

"The Lord is my shepherd; I shall not want. He makes me to lie down in green pastures; He leads me beside the still waters. He restores my soul; He leads me in the paths of righteousness For His name's sake. Yea, though I walk through the valley of the shadow of death, I will fear no evil; For You are with me; Your rod and Your staff, they comfort me. You prepare a table before me in the presence of my enemies; You anoint my head with oil; My cup runs over. Surely goodness and mercy shall follow me all the days of my life; And I will dwell in the house of the Lord Forever, Amen."

Those words pierced through my body like fire and allowed me to release the loudest outward cry I'd ever heard. It was a sound that came from so far down in me, that I felt I'd vomited it out of my belly. I began to tremble and sob, and Aunt Gloria sat at the head of my bed and held onto me like a boa constrictor that had captured its prey.

"Cry baby, let it out I am here. I have got you! I will not leave you I am not going anywhere. I love you, child and your life is not over. There is a plan for you and that baby that needs you. Nikki baby, cry it out. Give all your pain to the heavens, let it out."

She rocked my body back and forth, holding me and bringing me back to God.

It felt like we sat right in that spot for hours. She just let me cry and cry, reassuring me that she would not leave me in the state of pain I was currently in. I finally had a sense of sudden calm over me. I felt like the energy in my room was so serene, almost to the point it seemed surreal.

Aunt Gloria finally released me from her arms and sat in the chair next to my bed. She reached for her Bible and told me to lay down.

"I am here now. Relax, baby. You just rest." She sat in the chair and began to read scriptures out loud to me until nightfall.

It was in this moment when I knew I no longer wanted to die. Not only did I not want to end my life, I knew I would never allow life to pounce on me and defeat me to this magnitude again. I knew right then that there was a higher power higher than what I could comprehend. Only God could have pulled me out of that darkness. He was the only one who could have made me feel like I was really important and that my life mattered. He sent Aunt Gloria to remind me of that.

She left me that night feeling full of love like somebody in this world understood everything I was going through. She did what everyone else who'd come to see me couldn't do. She reminded me that there was a little life that needed me and I would need to be the best mother to her that I could possibly be. I could never abandon her ever again. Aunt Gloria encouraged me to apologize to the heavens for attempting to take my life, and to forgive myself for the thought of wanting to give up. If I had nothing, I had my baby girl to live for, and that was all I needed to go on.

The psychiatrist came in to see me the next day and I was in a totally different mental space than the day before. During our conversation, I spoke to her about knowing what I had to live for and that I no longer wanted to take my life. I told her when I left that hospital, I would give the life that I have all that is within me to give. I would succeed no matter how hard things may get or seem.

She smiled, relieved. She asked me several additional questions to satisfy her evaluation, and to be absolutely sure it was safe to report to the attending physician that I was doing much better. She shared that with me, and also mentioned that she would recommend that I be released from the hospital and no medication was needed. Before she left, she told me that the doctor would come in and speak with me and do his own evaluation before he would allow me to leave.

"I am glad you're feeling better, Nicole. Wait for the doctor to come by, but, in the meantime, order some lunch." She stressed to me that if I'm ever feeling overwhelmed or severely saddened again, to not hesitate to seek help. She reached inside of her pocket and handed me a card. I looked at it, and there was information on it about a suicide helpline that was available 24 hours a day, including holidays. I didn't have to feel alone in the world. There would always be someone there to speak with me during a time of crisis. Things were starting to feel better by the minute. I knew it would take some work to get myself back to happy again, but I had something that I hadn't had in a really long time. Hope.

As I waited for my lunch, the telephone rang.

"Hey Nikki, baby? How are you feeling?"

It was my grandmother. I smiled as she explained that she was sad that she was unable to come to the hospital. "I understand,

Granny. It's okay." For the first time in days, I worried about someone else. I knew she was trying to get back on her feet after her surgery, and I wanted to know that she was okay. I understood that no matter where she was, she loved me. If she could get to me, she would have. She always did.

Granny told me that Reverend Reed would be back to visit me later. I explained to her that the hospital psychiatrist had just left and I believed that the doctor would allow me to come home today since she thought I was doing much better.

She was so excited. "Baby, if they release you, I want you to have Reverend Reed bring you here to the house. I want you and that baby to live with me and your grandfather. I no longer want you out here living anywhere with that baby. We are here for you and we love you. We hope to see you later."

I agreed, said goodbye, and hung up the telephone. The idea of going to live with my grandparents gave me some peace. Things really felt like they were beginning to turn around for me. The doctor came by later that afternoon and officially discharged me. While I was waited on the nurse to come with my paperwork, Reverend Reed walked into my hospital room. He pushed the door closed behind him, leaving it just slightly cracked. He had a huge smile on his face.

"You are looking remarkably better than you were three nights ago when I saw you. God is so good!"

I explained that the doctor was allowing me to go home and that my grandmother wanted him to bring me to her house after I picked up all of my belongings and my baby girl from my friend's house.

He smiled again. "It would be my pleasure, darling."
Another angel. And another new chapter of my life.

The Naked Truth

You see, there is a possibility that, at some stage in life, you may experience emotional trauma. Or someone you know may experience a mental break or total meltdown like I did. Sometimes suicide seems like it's the only way out of that painful place that you or someone you care about may be in at the time. It never is.

We don't always know the source of our sadness or depression. It could be a mental imbalance that may have been in us since birth, or one caused by drugs of some kind. Or could have been bought on, almost out of nowhere, due to life's current circumstances. Life can easily overwhelm us, and leave us feeling as if there is no way to break free from the mental agony that we're experiencing. We can retreat to a very dark place, a place where no one can reach. When we get to that place, sometimes nothing, not even the calls of people we love the most, can pull us back. You can't think of anything or anyone else. You just want the heartache or headache to go away. For some people, suicide feels like their only way out.

Many may have thought, I was a strong girl. I had decided to keep my baby and I'd overcome the obstacle of fighting to graduate the way I did, giving it all I had and refusing to not see my dream become a reality. But there was so much more going on inside of me. What we see on the outside, at work, school, or even at a family gathering may be a cute little façade. It's easy to act. It's easy to smile through the pain. But I would go behind closed doors and there would be nowhere to run to or to hide. There was nobody watching me. It was just me and my truth.

If that has been you, know that you don't have to stay behind those closed doors in the darkness alone. My friend, trouble won't last always. While you may be standing in a dark place right now and you find yourself in that unfamiliar place down the road that may make you question whether or not to take your life, know that you should never choose suicide. Never choose a permanent solution to a temporary problem. Just when you think there is no way out, or no one who can help you, God sends that angel. There is always, always, someone there for you. Reach out for help. It's there. All you have to do is ask. People can't read our minds and sometimes they can't even read our actions. Even those closest to us. If there is something wrong, say it. Pick up the phone and call someone. Get in the car and drive to their house. Go to a church or hospital if you have to. Just get to someone.

The road that you may find yourself on may be pretty bumpy and rough, but remember this—you always have the option to change your direction to the road you wish to travel.

"I can do all things through Christ which strengtheneth me."
Philippians 4:13 (KJV)

4

CARELESS & RECKLESS

That day went something like this…

"911, what's your emergency?"

"Yes, ma'am, can you send the police to 9618 Ventura? I need the police at this location to help me to retrieve my belongings please."

"Sure, do you live at this location?"

"Yes, I do. My ex-boyfriend and I had a disagreement a few days ago and I am trying to get my stuff so I can move out, before he comes back home. I'm trying to keep the peace."

"Sure, what is your name?"

"Nicole, and I am occupying a silver Plymouth 4 door vehicle around the rear of the building. It's a little hard to find."

"Alright, ma'am, an officer will be there shortly."

I sat in my car in front of my boyfriend's apartment, shaking from both anger and fear. I hoped the police didn't take all day to get to me. I'd just had another big blowout argument with my daughter's father, and there was something about this time that felt like enough. I just wanted to get my stuff so I could be done with his crazy ass.

I breathed a sigh of relief when I saw the flashing lights from the police cruiser's silent siren. I got out of the car before he pulled up next to me, just to be sure he saw me and didn't leave. He pulled up, parked, and slowly got out of the car.

"Hello there ma'am. Nicole is it?"

I nodded. "Yes."

"Did you call the police?"

I nodded again.

"How can I help you?"

"Yes sir. I need your presence while I get my stuff out of my ex-boyfriends house."

I went on to explain that no one was home, but I had a key. The officer also asked how much "stuff" I needed to get from the apartment. There was two bedroom sets, one for me and one for my daughter, a kitchen table, and all of our clothing.

When I said furniture, his eyes widened.

"How are you going to get that?" he asked.

"Oh my friend is on her way with her cousin and a truck. They should be pulling up any second now."

"Do you have receipts for the furniture you will be removing from the home?"

I hadn't thought about that. I knew I'd purchased that furniture and clearly my clothes belonged to me. When I told the officer that I didn't have any receipts, but the items were definitely mine, he shook his head.

"I understand that, Nicole, but I can't allow you to remove items that aren't clear who they belong to unless you have receipt." He shrugged his shoulders as if there was nothing else he could do.

"Are you serious? Well can I at least get my clothes and my baby's clothes from out of that apartment?

"Sure, clothing items and things of that nature that are distinctly yours are not a problem for you to retrieve."

Accepting that I was just going to have to take this "L" and leave the furniture for now, I handed the officer my driver's license as he asked. At the same time, my girl Shay pulled up with her truck. I gave her the short and sweet version of what the officer had just shared with me, and that there had been a change in plans.

The officer, who'd been in his car for a while verifying my license I assumed, walked back over to me. I was hopeful that he'd found the information he needed so we could get into the apartment, get the clothes, and go. It had been a long day and I just wanted to get back to my aunt's house where I was planning to stay for a while until I got figure out how to get my own place.

> "Umm, Nicole, what is your correct date of birth and social security number?"

I sensed something wasn't right. I recited my date of birth slowly with an unsure look on my face, considering he had my Driver's License in his hand.

> "Is everything okay?" I asked.

> "Is the silver Plymouth you're occupying registered to you?"

> "Yes, sir, it is."

Everything around me started moving one hundred miles a minute.

"Ma'am, I need you to turn around and place your hands behind your back. You are under arrest for first degree vehicular assault."

I was so stunned I didn't know what to say. I couldn't believe what the officer had just said to me. I felt like I was moving in slow motion as I put my hands behind my back and he nudged me up against the car.

"I will be towing your vehicle. It was used as a weapon to commit a crime. I have to take you in for questioning. Once you get there you will speak to the detectives at the precinct, who are handling this case."

By this point I am crying hysterically and Shay is trying to keep calm, but she was just as scared as I was.

"Nikki, what do you want me to do?"

"Just get my baby from school and I'll call you as soon as I can."

As the officer placed me in handcuffs, I shook my head and looked him in his face.

"This is some bullshit, sir, I was the one in danger but okay. I know you are doing your job."

He opened the door to the back of the squad car and closed the door behind me after I slid across the seat. How in the hell did I get arrested and sent to jail? I thought as the car pulled away and the apartment faded in the distance.

I sat in a disgusting holding area at the county jail for almost eight hours. I hadn't had a sip of water or gone to the bathroom since morning. I knew that I was entitled to a phone call. I needed to call somebody to come and get me out of there. There was no way that I would spend the night in a cell. Especially for a crime I did not commit.

"Excuse me, Sir." I waved at the guard in the holding area, motioning for him to come over to the area I was sitting.

"Yes, can I help you?"

I knew I couldn't let my anger show if I had any chance to getting him to help me, so I was a polite as I could be.

"Yes, sir, can I make a phone call?"

"You have to wait for the arresting detective and they

will give you your phone call."

"Oh! Well do you know when they will be in to talk to me? I've been here for a long time without anyone talking to me yet."

"It shouldn't be much longer because they get off at 11 o'clock," he said as he walked away and went back to his desk.

If my eyes could create fire, I would have burned a hole right through his body. I was so mad! I couldn't hold all of my frustration in.

"Man, that's some bull!" I said to his back as he walked away. "Now this is just wrong!"

"Robinson, first name Nicole, please step to the counter."
Another guard called my name. I practically ran to the desk.

"Well, young lady," he started, "the arresting detectives are on their way and I need to place you in an interrogation room to be questioned."

Baby, with the ugliest mad face I could possibly make, I rolled my eyes. I watched the guard step down from behind the counter and shuffle a set of keys that hung from a thick, silver chain on his belt. He motioned for me to follow him into a room not far from the holding area.

"Don't look so mad," he said with this grin on his face.

All I could do was smile and shake my head from side to side. Nobody would believe I had been straight arrested and was in a damn jail as a suspect! Heck, I barely believed it.

How could I get myself in this type of mess? Damn, Nicole!

A woman walked in.

> "Hello Nicole, I am the detective that has been assigned to your case. Now before we get started I want you to know I have talked to Ms. Channel and the other young ladies that were with her and I have received their statements as it pertains to the incident in question. Now I want you to know I will be contacting any and all the people that were with you the night this incident occurred, so it would be in your best interest tonight to be honest with me about what happened on the night in question—"

Honey, baby, child, before that detective could get the end of her sentence out, I jumped in. "I'm not gonna lie!"

> "Okay, Nicole. That would be in your best interest. So I have to let you know this will be recorded, here we go."

As she started to read my Miranda rights, I thought to myself how strange it was to actually hear those words that most people only know from the movies.

> "Knowing and understanding your rights as I have explained them to you, are you willing to answer my questions without an attorney present?"

I felt so numb. I can't explain how I was really feeling, but, one thing's for sure, I wasn't scared. I knew I had not done anything wrong. With confident eyes, I looked up at that detective.

> "Yes I understand my rights and I'm ready to get this over with, ma'am. I don't need an attorney at this time."

> "Alright, Nicole. Can I please have the names of the people that were with you the night of the incident and their telephone numbers to contact them?"

> "Sure no problem."

I began to run down the list of names and numbers of the girls I was with that night. The detective wrote the information down on a large yellow legal notepad, and then she surprised me by leaning over and pulling the telephone that sat in the center of the table over to her.

So she's really going to call them? I started to panic. Not because I had anything to hide, but I didn't know what these chicks would say and if we would all have the same version of the truth. Everybody's loyalty was questionable when the cops got involved.

As I sat there with sweaty hands and a shaking knee, the detective dialed the first number on the list. I sat there as she asked questions about the incident and occasionally glanced up at me, while writing all kinds of stuff down on this notepad she had. I tried to read upside down with no freaking luck. By this time I'm on the edge of my chair, forehead wrinkled and with a puzzled look on my face, hoping my friend would speak up just a tad bit so I could hear something. Geesh, anything. I didn't want to be caught off guard when the detective turned her attention back to me.

After a lot of "umm hmm" and "Yes, I see…" on her end, she finally made her last call and hung up the phone. She jotted down a few more notes. I guessed I was next up on the interrogation list.

"Sit back and relax. Don't look so serious," she tells me with what feels like a fake smile. What the hell, she mean sit back and relax? Lady you trippin'. I'm sitting up in this interrogation room in a whole real jail under arrest. You are talking to my friends and I have absolutely no idea of what they are saying and you acting like this is a cakewalk.

All I could think about was how these situations typically play out in the movies. I sit in this box of a room for hours while this lady asked me the same questions forty different ways, trying to get me to crack. I would be dragged back to that funky cell until I got a bond hearing days later. I could see me in the orange jumpsuit, my Auntie crying in the courtroom, the whole nine...

I'm gonna need money on my books tonight!

My imagination was in overdrive. I started to run down a list of names in my mind, thinking about who I could really call if this thing went left.

The detective snapped me back to reality. "Well Nicole, now that I have a statement from all of the parties involved, will you please tell me what happened that night with the incident involving Ms. Channel?"

I let out a huge, exasperated sigh. Finally, I got to tell my side of the story.

Well here's the thing! So my friends and I were at the skating rink having a blast, I mean straight kickin' it. You don't understand. The music was poppin' that night.

Here we were minding our own business, and, now mind you, it was towards the end of the night and who makes sure I see them? Yes Ms. Channel, my ex-boyfriend's baby momma and some girls that were with her. So she walks past, looks me up and down with the stare of death, like she was the crypt keeper coming to collect a death wish that was placed on me."

"Okay," the detective says as she writes on her pad and nods.

So she says, 'Is there a damn problem?' I look back at her, unbothered, and said, 'I don't know is there?' I turned towards my friends and said 'It's 'bout time to bounce 'cause I don't even have time for her foolishness today,' because in the past she has always had something slick and sassy to say to me. But, you see, tonight seemed a bit different because she had a bit of an entourage to show out for. My friends and I made a v-line and headed straight for the door to leave. No sooner than when I got to the parking lot to my car, I see her and her friends walking rather swiftly. Might I add her car was parked across from mine coincidently? I think not. We went ahead and got into my car and drove off. I told my friends, while in the car, 'You know what y'all? I'm glad I decided to be done with that relationship with him because I don't have time for his abuse or his baby momma and her damn childish games. She acts as if I wanted to take her place in her son's life! Hell she's the one that is ratchet and unfit. It's not my fault her baby daddy took his son from her.'

So while I was riding down Interstate 70 to take my friends home, that crazy girl came speeding up to the rear of my car honking her horn and flashing her high beams on her car like she was a mad woman. My friend in the back seat turned around and said, 'Nicole that girl is following you and the other girls hanging out her convertible yelling something. They crazy as hell 'cause I knew they getting wet with this rain starting to come down. Just stupid.

I said, 'Yeah, she stupid and crazy. But she not 'bout to keep trippin' with me. Sit tight y'all, we 'bout to go by our apartment real quick before I take y'all home. I need to let him know he needs to handle this situation with his baby momma because if we are together or not, I don't have time to be beefin' with this silly girl!"

I began to speed up and I exited the interstate. No sooner than I put my blinker on, she put on her blinker and got right off the highway with me. I proceeded to drive to the apartment and sure thing she was right behind me. If I switched lanes, she switched lanes. I mean like a real maniac, so it was very apparent she was definitely following me. I speed up so I could make it through a yellow light. I went through it and sure 'nough, she missed the light and got caught at the red light. I continued on to the apartment and pulled up like I had swiftly. It was like lighting had carried my car. I came to an abrupt stop right in front of the door of the building at the grass edge. I didn't even park in a parking spot. I jumped out told my friends I would be right back.

I ran into the building and darted to the top of the steps, taking them two at a time to the apartment door. Totally out of breath, I beat on the door like I was the police. My ex came to the door, and before he could even say anything, I told him 'You better come and get your damn baby momma! She is crazy and I don't have time to be dealing with this girl, she started trippin' at the skating rink and she drove like a mad woman following me here.' Right as I was talking she arrived and began banging on the entry door to the building. He looked down the steps, and was like 'What the hell?'

One of his friends came out of the apartment because he heard all of the commotion. We all walked down stairs towards the door. His friend turned to me and said, 'Nicole, stand in here don't go out there yet.' I just wanted to get out of there. So I pushed the door open and began walking to my car. Ms. Channel charged at me, yelling all kinds of stuff. 'Bitch, you think you are the shit! You ain't my son's momma hoe, he got a momma!' As I turned to take a defensive stance, my ex grabbed her.

His friend stood between us all and said, 'Nicole, just gon' go, get in your car.' I walked to my car door, opened it, and told my friends it was time to roll. I started my car and Ms. Channel broke away from my ex, got to the front of my car, and began kicking the hood with these ridiculously hard, brown combat boots she had on. She was yelling, 'Nawl, hoe, don't leave. Get out the car! Get out the car!"

I opened my car door and stood in the doorway, while my friends sat nervously in the car. I said to her in the calmest voice possible, 'Can you please stop kicking my car? Look, I don't know what your deal is, but can you move out of my way so I can leave?'

She looked at me with her hands and arms waving in the air yelling, 'Bitch, you ain't going nowhere. You wanna leave bitch? You gon' have to move me.'"

"I sat back in my car and looked at her. Her two friends had now surrounded my car, one on the passenger side and one standing in the rear of my car. They were clearly willing and ready to be down for whatever she was down for.

My friend, Kay, asked what was I going to do. I sat there with my blood boiling and tension building, thinking about how these girls followed me home and now are threatening me. I yell again though the window, 'Girl just move out of my way!' I know she heard me because, for one, my driver side window was down and, for two, she responded with several more kicks to the front of my car's bumper and grill. She yelled and threatened again, 'Hoe you heard what I said! I ain't moving, so move me!'"

So I put my car in drive, stepped on the gas slightly and inched towards her, just trying to get her to move. I thought if I got her and her friend from the front and passenger side edge of my car, and I could go around her, I could pull off and leave. Well, hell, she didn't move.

She slammed her hands on the hood of my car and started laughing. 'Bitch, you scared, huh? You ain't gon' do nothing.' Then she raised her foot and kicked the grill one last time. I put my foot on the gas and it seemed like my car went from 0 to 30 in a matter of seconds. My car hit her and her body flipped onto the hood of my car like a shiny new Jaguar cat car ornament.

I firmly turned my steering wheel to the left, like my life depended on it. I drove the car up onto the grass in front of the building. I slammed on my vehicle brakes. Ms. Channel slid off the hood of my car and down the brick wall of the apartment building like a blob of slime from a Nickelodeon show and landed in one of the basement windows alongside the front of the building.

My friends were screaming, 'Oh My God! Oh My God! What the hell?!?!' I didn't even realize what had really happened in the moment. Everything was so chaotic and I was so scared. I looked at Ms. Channel looking back at me, I put my car in reverse, and drove away. And that is pretty much all that happened."

I took a breath for what felt like the first time since I started speaking. Recalling what happened that night brought up memories of one my friend Kay screaming, 'Lawd we some damn fugitives. We gone go to jail forever!!' as we pulled off. She was right, I thought. We are going to jail. Correction, I am going to jail.

"So, Nicole you didn't wait to see if she was alive?" the detective asked.

"No. I knew she was alive. She looked right at me with tears in her eyes which was a sure sign she was alive and in pain."

"Did anyone decide to call the police?"

"Well nobody in my car did. I guess they did later because she was hurt. I don't know." See, Detective, I promise I was not trying to hurt her. I was really trying to leave and she would not allow me to do that. I didn't have an issue with her, she apparently had an issue with me. If it means anything at all, I am really sorry it happened this way."

That wasn't a lie. I did not intentionally hurt that woman. I wasn't in the streets looking for her and plotting to get her if we ever ran up on each other or anything. Would we ever be friends? No. Did I want to kill her? Absolutely not.

"Do you understand the severity of this incident and what could have happened? Do you understand that this may not end well for you?

"Yes, I do." Not like I didn't know this was serious before, but I definitely knew it in that moment.

"I have everyone's statement of what happened that night, and I mean everyone's. To be honest they all sided with you, well except for Ms. Channel and her friends, of course. But even with their statements, they seemed too rehearsed as if they all were telling the same lie. Just so you know your friends said pretty much exactly what you said but from their position in the car. It was pretty damn funny because they didn't lie for you. That normally doesn't happen and I mean ever."

That made me feel somewhat better. I knew I wasn't lying, and I didn't think my friends would not tell the truth, but I was still terrified that this woman had already decided I was guilty and nothing that anyone said would change her mind.

"I am going to release you, and there will be a court date to see if Ms. Channel wants to prosecute you in this matter."

"So I'm free to go tonight?"

"Yes, you are free to go. You can get information from booking about your vehicle and how you can get it from the pound. I will send over the release order for it."

I sat there in disbelief, unsure of how I was just released from jail without an attorney and walked away without being charged with a crime. At least not yet. This was all so crazy. And I even felt crazy. But I was thankful.

It felt like a dream when I walked into the county courthouse two weeks later for my hearing. Being in a jail was one thing, but being in a courtroom was something different. All of the air was sucked out of me when I walked in there. I had never been in trouble with the law before. The detective who questioned me walked in, in front of me and motioned for me to sit on the left side of the courtroom. I looked around and noticed Ms. Channel was sitting there with one of the girls that were with her that night. She had a pair of crutches sitting beside her, a full cast on her leg, and one of her arm with a soft sleeve on it. Seeing her made me feel horrible about everything that happened. I could barely look her way, and I noticed she avoided eye contact with me too, as if she was embarrassed about her actions.

The judge walked in and the clerk ordered us to stand until he was seated. I sat there thinking about how scared I was. And that fear was growing by the minute. I was terrified that this girl would get up there and tell the judge her story and, if she presented it as if I was guilty, he would believe her. The magnitude of all of this began to hit me again. My fate, my life, was in somebody else's hands. I felt super nauseated and vomit started to rise up in the back of my throat.

The judge asked the state appointed attorneys to approach the bench to speak with him. When they were done, the judge asked Ms. Channel to stand.

"Due to your injuries, I won't have you step forward," he said. "Is it of sound mind and without coercion that you have come to the conclusion that you do not wish to prosecute in this case?"

With assurance, she uttered the greatest words I'd ever heard in my life.

"Yes, your honor, I do not wish to press charges."

"If that is your stance, then I hereby call this case closed and adjourned."

My God, I wanted to fall to my knees. I was just minutes away from going to jail. From not being able to hold my daughter. From being defined as a criminal for the rest of my life. I was spared. I was free.

Standing there in that courtroom, at that very moment, I realized how easy it was for me to let a temporary moment of anger completely change the course of my life. I handed my life over to someone else to decide my fate. In the heat of that horrible night, I couldn't see past what was happening at the time, never giving my future or my baby girl's future a second thought as so many of us do. I had been careless and reckless with my life. I couldn't ever do that again.

I was at the edge of a ledge, about to fall, and someone or something extended me a rope to grab onto. I grabbed it and never looked back!

The Naked Truth

One thing I learned that day and I will never forget it—an unhealthy situation doesn't change unless something in it changes. For me, the change was for me to leave. I knew after that incident that the relationship I had one foot in and one foot out of was not a good environment for me mentally or emotionally. The incident with my ex's baby's mother really had nothing to do with us—it was a piece of a much larger puzzle. A symptom of a much bigger problem. This man was mentally and physically abusive and had heightened controlling tendencies. I don't even think he realized any of that was an issue at the time of our relationship. It took that incident for me to really see him and the situation for what it was. And I was forced to see me for who I was.

If you are in a situation, a relationship of any kind, that God has shown you, time and time again, that needs to change, I want you to do that. Today. Make the changes you need to make to save your life, to begin to heal your soul and spirit, to take your fate back into your own hands. I don't want you to wait for the legal system to set you free. Even if you've made some mistakes. Even if you've hurt people. Grab hold of that rope that is being held out for you so you don't fall off of that ledge of life.

"Have mercy upon me, O God, according to thy lovingkindness: according unto the multitude of thy tender mercies blot out my transgressions."
Psalm 51:1 (KJV)

5

TO HAVE & TO HOLD

t feels like Déjà vu. We'd only been married for six years, and we'd already been down this road before. Once again, I found out you've been dealing with someone outside of our marriage. Not once, but twice. And that's just what I know of.

There's the part of me that does not trust you right now, while the other half of me still wants to save my marriage. So before I get into what I need to say, I need you to know I still love you and I want my marriage. But I feel we need to separate. I think some time apart will allow us to gain some clarity about where we are in this relationship. We need to decide how we can save it or if we think it's worth saving at all. I just need to know one thing.

Are you willing to leave or do I need to?

Those were the words that started it all. Words that I held in me for so long, but had to be set free. If I didn't, I would stay stuck in this cycle of pain, hurt, disrespect, and unhappiness that was killing a piece of me, slowly, day by day. I didn't know what he would say or do next, but I knew what I needed to do.

I needed to create some space. I needed to find a quiet corner that I could go into and just breathe and hear myself. I needed to be away from him.

I should have known he would not make that easy.

"Nicole, I will tell you right now, I'm not going anywhere. I'm not leaving my home, so do what you feel is necessary."

"Okay! No need to make that a big deal about this. That is fine. The kids and I will leave!

Now with that being said, I have written down a list of things I feel we, not me or just you, need to work on to hopefully help get us back on track to having a healthy, happy, and trusting marriage again. I hope you can sit here and listen to this list with an open mind so we can discuss it and even add to this list if you think I missed something."

He didn't cut me off so that was a good sign. At least he was willing to hear me out. I don't know where I found all of this poise from. I had every right to go Tasmanian Devil-ess and tear that house to shreds—and him too. But there was something that kept me calm. Something that reminded me to keep my emotions in check so that I could be clear. And understood.

> "Here are the things on the list: Number One, the lying and dishonesty need to stop. Number Two, We need to communicate better."

I looked up briefly to glance at him. His face was blank, which means there was steam building beneath the hood. I put my head down and kept reading.

> "Three, there has to be accountability for the money made and where it is going. Four, we need to be a united force when disciplining the children. Five, defining what our roles are in this marriage, meaning what you will handle and what I will handle. Six, saying and doing what we say we will do. Seven..."

> "Wait a minute, Nicole, I don't need you to read the list to me like I am a child. I just read it for myself."

> "Oh! I'm sorry. Sure, here you go."

I walked over to the other side of the room, handed him the paper, and resumed my place on the couch, legs crossed, while he read.

> "Did I miss anything?" I ask impatiently. "Would you like to add anything to what I've written?"

He looks up at me with the no-her-ass-didn't look on his face. "No!"

> "Okay, I just want to add that during this time, although we are apart, we are still very married and need to be mindful of that fact. Also, since you are unwilling to leave, I will be moving into an apartment. And just so we both understand what that looks like, it

locks me into a one-year lease agreement. So we have approximately one year to fix what is broken in our marriage. I believe we should use this time apart to find where our hearts are with one another and for our marriage. Also, we need to communicate with one another in regards to addressing the issues on this list."

I couldn't read his mind, at least not exactly. There was pissed mixed with disbelief. "Hey, I know this may seem a bit all of a sudden, especially since we just celebrated Christmas with our families and our children, but that's just it, I'm tired of pretending. I am really unhappy and I'm sure you can tell. We really don't talk much, we don't do things together anymore, we are not barely having sex and you walk around here as if things are fine or either you don't want to talk about our problems. This just isn't what I saw for my marriage."

I wanted him to say something. Tell me he wanted to fix it too. That all of this was a mistake. That he knew how broken we were and how unhappy I was. Tell me he still loved me.

"Is there anything at all you want to say about what I've said or maybe didn't say at this point?"

"Nope, I have nothing to say."

Of course you don't have anything to say, I thought to myself. He sat there with the same blank-ass look on his face, like what I said went right over his head. This was exactly the problem. This man didn't care about anything. He could never make an adult decision without it being a total screw up!

"Okay, well, do you even agree that the separation is a good idea?"

"I think some time apart may be a good thing, and it could allow us time to look at some things that have gone awry in this marriage."

At least he had something to add to this conversation. This was like talking to a brick wall.

"Good. I'm glad we are on the same page about the separation then. Just one more thing, during this time if at any time you feel it's over, please let me know. There is no need to prolong the inevitable of a divorce."

"Just so you know, I don't plan on getting a divorce!"
"That's a good thing because neither do I!"

Finally we could agree on something.

"My mother will be bringing the kids back home later and I haven't said anything to them about this. I thought it would be best if we told them together about the separation. With it happening in the middle of the school year we need to assure them everything will be okay," I said.

He nodded and exhaled. There it was. We were separated.

A week later, I'd signed a lease for an apartment. The kids were on holiday break, and I wanted to get moved and settled before they went back to school. When I told my husband about my plans, he was shocked. I told him the truth. Moving fast was best for the kids and for us. The sooner we started fixing our marriage, the sooner things could get back on track.

We'd already sat down with our girls and told them what was happening. Speaking to them together was the best thing we could have done. It assured them that we all would be okay, and it made me feel that there was some real hope for keeping our family together. My husband wanted to be sure that he would still be able to see the girls whenever he wanted, and I promised he could. I wanted our daughters to feel secure that their father would always be there for them, as he always had. I wouldn't do anything to change that.

I moved the first weekend in January. It was like I looked up after Christmas, and, all of a sudden, I had a new life. My mom and aunt came over to help me unpack, and I was so grateful. Not just for the extra hands, but more for the support. I needed as much love around me as I could get.

"Momma and Auntie, I love ya'll so much for coming over today and helping me and the girls get settled."

"Oh Niecy, you're welcome! You know if yo momma was coming, I was gonna come with her to help. We know you are a bit O.C.D. and you must have the whole darn house unpacked the same day you move in!"

"Ha ha, you're not funny, Auntie," I said as I lowered my voice, not wanting my girls to hear me. "I just can't stand the boxes everywhere. Too much clutter and, with this move in particular, I just wanted things in order since the girls go back to school Monday from Christmas break. I want everything to be as normal as possible since we are in a new environment and keeping the circumstances in mind."

"So now, Nikki, you know Auntie don't get in your business because you are grown. But what actually happened for you to have to leave your house, babe?" My momma chimed in. "Tuh! Listen to this mess. You're not gonna believe it!"

"Momma, wait. I'll tell her." I know my mother was fighting the urge to say more. In fact, I was shocked she hadn't told the story before now. I was glad that we'd gotten to a point in life where I could talk to her and confide in her. She knew I was just as close to my Auntie, and that eventually I would share everything with her in my own time.

"Auntie, since we've been married, it's just been issue after issue. Money ain't right, he be lying all the time about stupid stuff like the bills and money he made at work. And on top of all that, he has been dealing with two different women. I caught him."

Oh but you have not heard it all. Auntie did not blink an eye. But there was more.

Now one of the women was someone I considered my friend. I mean the kind of friend you would have in the delivery room with you when you give birth. And then this other woman, OH MY GOD! He had the nerve to have nude photos on our family computer of this chick and when I found them, he said nothing happened. That he had recently met her at the damn gas station.

Now I understand things may happen in a marriage and things won't always be great. Auntie, but really, it's just too much. And on top of that I am carrying him and our home financially and trying to be a mother and wife. I told him I needed him to get another job at least to help get us out of the hole we are in with bills. He told me he had a job and he wasn't getting another one. I am overworked with no help. I don't trust nothing he says because he's such a liar. Heck, he can tell me it's raining I will go to the window and check for myself because he lies that much.

Both my mom and aunt chuckled a little at that one. I giggled myself, but I was serious as a heart attack. I did not trust this man. Period. And there was no way I could continue to live with someone who I could not count on to tell me the truth. About anything.

I went on. "Everything he says is always so embellished, like he painting a masterpiece for a big exhibit and he gotta make it sound good!"

My mother just shook her head, while my aunt sat there with

this disgusted look on her face, trying to chew up the bits of food she had in her mouth. She sat her sandwich down slowly onto a paper towel next to her 7-Up soda can, fresh out of the freezer, that still had ice shavings on it. It was the little things that still made her happy and it was my pleasure to take care of her in any way I could.

"What the hell you mean a 'friend' of yours, Niecy? And another woman?" She sat up straight with her hand grabbing onto her flowing, maxi skirt to pull it up from around her ankles, as she kicked her red slide on sandals off her feet. "Now let me get this straight. He messes around with a friend of yours and you stay with him?"

"Yes, this was when the baby was about one or two years old."

Then after that, you mean to tell me you stayed with his ass and he turns his trifling ass around again and deals with some other woman outside of your marriage?"

I felt embarrassment come over me when she said that. I knew my aunt was speaking out of outrage at my husband and not judgement of me, but it still hurt to hear someone question why I would give him yet another chance. Especially her.

> "That is exactly what I am saying, and this is why I needed us to take a break to re-evaluate this relationship. Auntie, my momma knows all of this. I asked her to not say anything to anyone."

My aunt turned to my mother. "You think this shit is okay? Him cheating on her and got her and them kids over there struggling like this? Now I know why every time this girl can't come to no family gatherings because she working. You mean his ass be at home? Oh hell nawl!"

My mom placed her hands on either side of her head and closed her eyes tight, as if her head was about to explode from stress. "Now Sis, I know you're upset. Lower your voice. The girls are upstairs, you know. But to answer your question, heck no I don't like it, and I don't like seeing her in the situation either. But it is Nicole's decision and life and I can't make it for her."

I moved the last empty kitchen box out of the way to distract myself. I felt tears burning my eyes and I fought hard to hold them back.

Auntie did not let up. "Why are you staying or even trying to make something work with a man who treats you this way?"

That was it. The lump in my throat. And then the tears came. I sobbed, hard, but tried to suppress the sound of my cry so my daughters wouldn't hear me. I looked at the two women in my kitchen. "You wanna know why I'm gonna try to make this marriage work? I'll tell you why. It's because the God in me said I can't leave yet. There is something I need to learn in this situation."

They both opened their mouths at the same time to speak.

I put up my hand so they would let me finish. "It sounds crazy, I know, but listen. Here's the thing. When I got with this man, from the very beginning he was a married man and I held on to him anyway. I left him alone for a minute. I wanted my own man, but ended up back with him after he continued to pursue me. Now when I got back with him, he and his wife split up and we got back together before their divorce was final. Yes, our marital foundation was weak based on how we started, but the marriage covenant is good and blessed."

By the look on both of their faces, neither Momma or Auntie were fully in agreement with me. But they let me keep talking.

"I feel this is my test for how I entered into a relationship with this man. I have all of this heartache right now because I didn't wait on God's husband for me. I understand that infidelity is grounds to get a divorce, but how hypocritical would I be to say you can cheat with me but not on me? On top of that, do you understand this is my baby girl's father? No, I shouldn't be mistreated for the sake of my children's happiness, but what would you do?"

I didn't give them a chance to answer, afraid of what the answer may be. "I am a fatherless daughter. My father was never around, and my oldest daughter's father is nowhere to be found. This man is the only father that she has known since she was three years old and she is now sixteen. So me just up and getting a divorce without trying to make it work on my end first doesn't just mean that baby girl loses the chance to be raised in a two-parent household and with her father, but now my oldest will also not have a father yet again."

My mother handed me some tissue to wipe my messy face. "From where I sit, I would rather try all that is within me, so, if and I mean a MIGHTY BIG IF, a divorce is to be had then I will have no guilt with my girls or before God that I didn't try all that I could to keep my family together."

I could tell from the silence that they were skeptical. These women loved me and their protection of me was fierce. Anyone or anything that hurt me or my girls in any way was unacceptable to them, and I loved them for that. Maybe I should have decided then to not give my husband and my marriage another chance, but the devotion to creating a loving family for my children was real. If I was going to fight for my marriage, then I had to give it all I had. That was my truth.

Over the next few months, my husband and I remained separated and while the communication between us was rocky, we were both committed to being the best parents we could for the girls. He saw them regularly, and we spent some holidays together. I felt like things were at least moving in the right direction. But I knew only time could tell.

I was riding down the street one day, just leaving home on my way to work, in a great mood. It was rush hour and traffic was getting crazy, but I felt good, light and free. A mix of some of my favorite songs was blasting, and I was jamming! I barely heard my cell phone ringing in my purse next to me.

I snatched up the phone on what had to be the last ring before it went to voicemail. I saw my daughter's number flash across the screen. "Hey, babe. What's up?" I yelled over the music. I hear her crying uncontrollably and screaming at the top of her lungs. Panic sets in.

"Wait what? What's wrong? Let me turn the radio down I can't hear you. Hold on."

She starts to lose it. "Ma, I knew it, I knew it! I knew he was lying!" She can barely get her words out through her sobs.

I try to get her to calm down. "What? Hold on, what are you talking about?"

"Ma, Dad is a liar! He told us this lady was just a friend and he wants his family back together and crap but this lady is more than that. I knew I wasn't crazy and now I have proof."

My mind started racing with possible scenarios about what had happened. I knew my girls were supposed to be getting their hair done at the salon where their father worked, and my first priority was making sure they were there and safe. "Proof? Baby, what proof? Wait, where are you? Where is your baby sister?"

"I'm at the salon. She is in the salon and I'm outside. I asked if I could use his phone to download some music and he said 'yes.'"

I didn't let her finish. I needed to get to her. "Okay, wait, I'm getting off the highway to come there. Give me a second, and I'll be there in a few minutes. Just sit tight, baby and calm down."

I veered off the interstate and on to Goodfellow Boulevard, accelerating from 30 miles an hour to 55 in a residential area. The anger was building inside of me. Not only were we supposed to be working on this farce of a marriage, my baby was crying, telling me she caught you in a lie. After all I'd put up with and done to keep my kids out of our mess, and this is what happens? I was furious. I started driving like a maniac, beeping my horn at cars sitting in the middle of the street or not moving fast enough, all while talking myself off of an emotional ledge that could lead to me doing something irrational if I didn't check myself.

'Okay, calm down Nicole. Calm down. Don't jump to conclusions! You haven't got the whole story yet,' I told myself.

I pull up to a red light, and say a quick prayer. "Thank you God for giving me a red light to calm my butt down."

I pull up to the front of the hair salon and my daughter is still standing outside, visibly upset and crying. Seeing her like that lit a fresh fire in me.

I ran over to her and she falls into my arms, hysterical. I try to console her. "Now tell me what happened. And please calm down, stop crying, babe. Here take this napkin and wipe your face."

She tries her best to control herself long enough to speak. "Well, I asked to use his phone for music or whatever, and while I was out here downloading my songs, his phone started to get some messages. At first I ignored them, but then the phone kept going off. Momma, I know I should not have looked at the messages because it was none of my business. But I checked anyway and I see all these messages about some trip they took last week. Now we know why he didn't come and get us. He was with her!"

I listen and keep urging her to relax. I knew I needed to hold my emotions in check for her. But on the inside, I am ready to lose my mind. "It's okay, baby, stop crying."

"No, Ma. He not only has messages from this lady, Candy, or whatever. There are messages from somebody else he is supposed to meet for dinner tonight somewhere. I just don't understand why would he say he wants his family back and turn around and be talking to other ladies." My girl was devastated. And there was nothing I could do about it.

As I grab my baby and comfort her, feelings of guilt come over me. This is the reason why I wanted to leave. I could not trust this man to honor me or our marriage, and now my daughter, our daughter, was a causality of his careless behavior and deceit. The sadness inside of me kept building, and slowly becomes rage. All I could think of was needing to guard my babies heart from hurt. That was my number one job in this life.

I needed to see this with my own eyes, so when I confronted him about all of this, I would have every fact necessary. "Where is the phone now? Let me see what you saw."

She hands me his phone, and I tap the message icon and start to scroll quickly. There were sexy photos that no wife would want to find in her husband's phone, followed by some other messages between him and a woman about spending quality time and conversations about sex. I handed the phone back to my daughter and told her go inside and get her sister. I didn't want them in there when I went inside. A few minutes later, the girls come back out. I kiss my eldest on the forehead, give my baby a quick hug, and tell them to get in the car. I walked into the salon and made a straight v-line towards my husband's work station. The look on his face told me that he knew I didn't come for pleasantries.

"So while I think we are working on our marriage, you are dating huh? I mean you're not only dating one lady, you got two on yo' phone line, right?"

He had a client sitting in the barber chair. He turns the chair away from me, turns off his clippers, and the entire salon seemed to get super quiet. He looks me up and down, slowly, and gives me nothing but a challenging "Bitch, bye. And what you gonna do about it if I do?" stare.

I raised my eyebrow and cocked my head, giving him an "Oh really?" look in return.

He hung up his clippers, and, before I knew it, I pulled my right arm back and swung it forward with a balled fist as if I needed the strength to knock down a mountain with that punch. I tried to take his head off his body. I followed it with my left arm coming straight up to strike another blow to his body. He walked around me and headed for the front door.

I was right on his heels and caught him right before he opened the door. "Look, don't go outside. The girls are out there. Let's not do this in front of them. Just tell me. Did I not say if this was not what you wanted to tell me. We could have just gone on living our lives and gotten the divorce."

He just stood there, clearly trying everything he could to suppress his anger. He looks at me, says nothing, and storms outside to the car. He yanks the drivers side door open and yells at my oldest daughter, "Give me my phone!"

When she didn't move fast enough for him, he reaches in and snatches it out of her hands.

Did he just put his hands on my daughter? I thought. I wasn't having it. "Don't yell at her! Why are you mad at her 'cause you are caught? And by a child this time, not me?"

"You don't know what the hell you're talking about."

"Oh really? I don't? Well guess what, I can read well and I read what she saw." I grab for the top flip part of the phone. "Come on, let's read it together since I don't know what I'm talking about. You can explain it."

He exploded. He turned, grabbed me, and slams me onto the hood of my car. The phone broke in two pieces.

He and I tussle as he reaches to pry the phone from my hands. Meanwhile, my oldest daughter jumps out of the car.

"Dad, why would you do that? Why you hitting Mom, banging her head on the car hood? Why are you doing this?" She lunges at him to try to protect me while my baby girl cries in horror in the backseat.

It was a mess. My husband walks back into the salon, leaving the three of us in front of the shop, with Lord knows who watching. I was stunned and just trying to process what just happened.

The man who was in my husband's chair when I arrived comes out of the salon and over to the car. My guess is that he watched the entire scene from the door. Now that I had a chance to see him again, I recognized him as the owner of the building where the shop was. He was a very influential and well-known man in the city. He walked over to me with a concerned look on his face.

"Go inside and get you all's things," I tell my daughter.

As I am standing there talking to my husband's client, who wanted to be sure I was okay, my husband comes back outside. He was talking on the phone, and from what I could piece together from the conversation, I gathered that he was talking to the police. I couldn't believe him!

His client walks over to him and convinces him to hang up the phone.

"This is a personal matter," he said to both of us. "Nicole, you are out here in your police uniform," he pointed out. He was right. I was in uniform and, to his point, did I want my co-workers in my personal business? No. But in the moment, I was too heated to think about that. "So I'm not at work," I responded.

"I know, but this is something that can be handled at home later."

My husband and I stood there staring each other down, My daughter put the last of their things in my car handed me the keys.

"Drive you and your sister home," I told her. She seemed confused as to why I was not coming with them, and I know, after seeing what she just saw, she was scared to leave me for fear of what her father may do. She started to cry again.

"Don't cry, baby. Everything will be alright. I want you and your sister to go straight home. I will see you later," I assured her.

She strapped her baby sister in her car seat, got back in the driver's seat and drove off.

While my husband stood there ranting with his client about me, I walked angrily over to our truck that he'd parked in a lot adjacent to the salon building. I climbed up into the driver's seat, and as he approached me, I heard him on the phone with what had to be the police based on the information he was giving. He ran down everything, my name, the fact that I was an officer and what district I was in, and my department.

This bastard... I couldn't believe he would do that. I started up the truck.

Panic struck his face. "Nicole, your not taking my truck!" he yelled as he reached in and tried to pull me out of the driver's seat.

> "Oh, really?" I shouted back. "Watch me. You are three months behind on the payments and this car is on my credit, but you don't give a damn. Have one of yo' women pick you up," I said with a sarcastic tone.

> "Since you have several to choose from, wit' yo cheating ass." I added.

He jumped on me, trying to pull the key from the ignition. It had to be every bit of 110 degrees in the vehicle since it had been sitting in the sun for hours. We were both sweating by this point, and he had a tight grip on my shirt and bullet proof vest that I wore underneath. I began to just pull away from him holding the key tightly in my fist so he couldn't take it.

He didn't give up. "You are not taking my truck, Nicole!" "Get off of me! You are hurting me! Let me go, dammit. Let me go!" I paused practically between every word, out of breath from wrestling with this man, while trying with all my might to hold onto the center console in the truck so he could not pull me out of the vehicle.

I threatened to mace him if he didn't get off of me. But he wasn't fazed. With what seemed like all 240 pounds of his body, he pressed me into the seat. Holding on to what felt like dear life, I released one hand from the center console to reach for my mace canister that was positioned on my police duty belt. He saw what I was trying to do, and grabbed my neck in an effort to snatch me from the car, but my grip was too strong. I was able to release to short burst of mace from the canister and it landed directly on the side of his face and neck. But instead of forcing him off of me, he leaned in with more of his body weight to try to pin me down. I inhaled the toxic fumes right along with him.

Struggling to breathe, I used all of my strength to pull my body over the center console. I moved further away from him and inched closer to the passenger side door.

"I can't breathe!" I screamed, reaching for the door to try to get some fresh air to flow into the vehicle.

He reached over and grabbed me, throwing me back. "I don't care about you being able to breathe, you can die for all I care."

I heard the sound of a police brigade of sirens getting closer and closer. He did too. He instantly let me go as I coughed violently from the mace.

Within seconds, I was able to breathe and felt fresh air filling my lungs. I climbed out of the truck, and there were at least seven police cars speeding up the road, including an unmarked detective vehicle. They all screeched up to the lot, surrounding us, with sirens blazing so loud. Policeman, supervisor Sergeants, and Lieutenants hopped out of their vehicles and ran toward us. One officer grabs my husband and puts him in handcuffs quickly. Another Detective and his partner from the Gang Unit walk over to me. I recognized them both.

"Hey, babe, you good?"

"Yeah, I'm good now." I was shook up and weak, but I was okay.

"Are you sure? You know they put an all-out "Officer In Need Of Aid" call out on you because a man on his porch across the street called in after your husband did. The man said a female police woman was fighting a man in a truck at this location. We all knew it was you. Your husband gave the dispatcher your whole damn name and what district you worked in, so we knew it was you, girl."

I was pissed all over again.

"If you're good, then we are out of here. We wanted to make sure you were good."

"I appreciate you two. Thanks." I said gratefully.

After all of the cars began to clear out, I sat there in disbelief. Maybe it was the craziness of the moment, but it didn't even feel like I had just been in a brawl with my husband. For some amazing reason, it felt like I'd released some weight off of me that I'd been carrying for years. All of the anger, all of the hate, all of the hurt, pain, disappointments in my marriage, and embarrassment of all that he has put me through. All of it felt like it had left my body, right there in that parking lot. My hands that had been shaking as we fought settled and my breathing returned to normal. The blazing heat from what felt like the hottest day in July didn't feel like it was suffocating me and even the sun seemed brighter. It was if the world opened up along with my soul. The struggle, in every sense of the word, was over.

A complete feeling of calm came over me and I knew right then that my marriage was now over. I knew I was filing for a divorce and ALL had been forgiven in that tussle I had just had! All of the guilt that I carried throughout our marriage about dealing with a man who already had a wife and how his infidelity was somehow punishment for me. For nine years I carried that sadness, heartbreak, and pain. And yes, I finally accepted that his decision to cheat on me, over and over again, was ultimately his. But the decision to stay and endure it? All mine.

At some point, I had to take responsibility for some of our issues and what I allowed him to do to me. I didn't know I was worthy of not being cheated on. I had never been truly loved, honored, and respected by any man in my life, so I didn't expect it from my husband. I knew what type of man he was when I met him, but I married him anyway. I accepted his disrespect, mistreatment, abuse, and lies because, deep inside, I felt like he was all I deserved. It didn't matter that I was the mother to two beautiful girls. It didn't matter that I was a smart, professional woman. It didn't matter that I worked so hard to make sure we all had nice things, and that I kept my hair done or people told me how beautiful I was, inside and out. None of that mattered because the Nicole I saw, the Nicole I knew, didn't know how valuable she was, or how worthy she was of the love she deserved. The deep-rooted skeletons of rejection and abandonment from all of the men in my past lives, starting with my father, had to come tumbling out of the closet. It was time to clean those closets for good.

So I did.

The Naked Truth

Sometimes we have to be brutally honest with ourselves—about everything. The people we allow to gain access to our hearts and our lives. The decisions that we've made. The disrespect we've accepted. The denial of the red flags that we chose to turn our backs to. Even when people show us who they are, more often than not, we don't believe them. At least not the first time. We want to love them and be loved past all of the pain of our pasts. We want to believe that with enough time and patience, they'll change. We want the fairy tale that we imagined we'd have. So we stay too long. We lose too much of ourselves. We do not deal with our truth.

My Love, the person who you have been waiting for months, maybe years, to change is not. But the person who you are can. Unpack all of the guilt and shame that you've been carrying, and fill those bags with your beauty and God's grace. Oh, and don't forget your love. You've left enough of that behind. Keep it for someone special, someone who deserves it. And for today, that person is you.

"Because of his strength will I wait upon thee: for God is my defence. The God of my mercy shall prevent me: God shall let me see my desire upon mine enemies."

Psalm 59:9-10 (KJV)

NICOLE M. BENTLEY

6

DANCE WITH THE DEVIL

"It's getting late. I better be going, baby."

I shifted the covers on the bed that covered my naked body and turned to look at the clock on the nightstand. It was 12:45 a.m. By the time I rolled back over to his side of the bed, he was already up, putting on his underwear.

This is the part I hate, I thought to myself.

I never liked to see him leave. The few hours that we were able to spend together, mostly in bed, was never enough. But I could pretend, just for a little while, that what we had was normal. That this man loved me and I loved him. That I wasn't sharing my body and heart with a married man. I wanted, I needed, something more.

"I really wish you could just stay with me most nights."

He turned around and looked at me while he pulled his shirt on. "Aww, baby, me too. But we can't think about that now, can we?"

"Yeah you're right. I'm just having one of my bratty

moments 'cause I don't want you to go home to her. You don't even want to be there, for real." I believed him when he said that he didn't want his wife anymore. Even though we'd been in a relationship all of this time, long enough for a man who was really done with his marriage to end it. But he never did.

"Nicole, stop it. You are just going to upset yourself. We've had a good evening, so let's not change the mood, okay?" He kissed me on my forehead as I lay there on the bed, wrapped in a sheet, looking like a sad puppy. This is what always happened whenever I tried to bring up what was going on between us and anything related to his other life. He shut it down immediately with some sweet talk or some other deflection from the truth. But this hurt me. And I wanted to talk about it with him. All of the time. But there was always a little part of me that was afraid to rock the boat too much. He was right, the time we spent together had been good. Always was. Did I want to push for more? Yes. But I knew that would come with risk. And a cost.

I decided to let it go. For now. "Okay. Will you be by here tomorrow?"

"Umm, I doubt it."

"Why not?" I asked.

"What is tomorrow, Nicole?" There was an irritation in his voice as if I should know better than to ask.

"It's the 14th and what does that mean?"

"I came over here today and stayed all day so I didn't have to hear your mouth tomorrow."

I sat up in the bed with an "I don't give a damn" look on my face. "So I had my Valentine's Day today, huh? So you have plans for tomorrow with her?"

"No, I don't! She doesn't want to do anything anyway. She asked for new carpet so that's what I gave her."

"So again you're not coming because of what?"

"How will that look me not being at home with my wife on Valentine's Day?"

It was moments like these when the imaginary bubble burst. When I could see this for what it was. I loved a man who loved me—and his wife.

"It will look like a man that ain't at home."

"Look I don't care about the hows, whys, and explanations. You wanted this relationship over here and you feel you will never have to sacrifice a few special days ever?"

"Yeah, you're right. Stay at home, be nice, and act faithful. I'm good." I smiled slyly. While I wanted to spend my Valentine's Day with him, I knew that I wouldn't spend it alone. It was just a matter of deciding who, I would spend it with. "I'll be respectful and play my position."

I leaned to give him a kiss. Satisfied, he patted my behind and headed towards the door. I threw on a robe and tied it as I walked him out. We said our goodbyes, kissed again, and he was gone. And just like always, I leaned against the other side of the door, already feeling lonely as if he'd never been there. The sadness that came with missing him whenever we were apart and the stupidity that came with falling in love with a man that would never be completely mine. Both consequences of a truth I refused to face.

The anger started to rise. But not at myself where it belonged. It was easier to blame him.

Every year, it's the same thing. Things gotta change! I thought to myself. That was true, something did need to change. I was tired of spending most nights, holidays, and special occasions by myself. I wanted a complete relationship which meant that I needed a man who was completely available to me. But as usual, I figured out how to rationalize what was happening in my mind, talking myself out of ending this so I could find what I knew I really wanted.

Girl, shit, snap out of it. You knew what this was when you started. I said to myself then took my butt to bed.

I woke up the next morning to the repetitive buzz of my cell phone vibrating against the wood shelf in my headboard. Without fully opening my eyes, I patted around for my phone and looked at the screen with squinted eyes. The flurry of expected texts had started to come in.

First, there was "Mr. Can't Get Right," the barber, with his lying self. He must be on his way to the shop.

"Happy Valentine's Day Beautiful," his message read, followed by two big red heart emojis. "I got plans to see you tonight."

I rolled my eyes. Yeah, okay. Instead of saying that, I responded with, "Hey! Thank You. Good Morning!" I kept scrolling.

Next up was "Mr. Railroad" with his missing-in-action ass. I was shocked that he even bothered to send anything. It had been weeks since I'd heard a peep outta him. But just thinking about him bought a smile to my face.

Damn, that boy fine as hell and his body? Oh, lawd! He ain't shit, but he does have potential and not any real baggage, so I gots to kick it wit' him! LOL!

I texted back. "Hey, You. Good Morning. Thank you for thinking of me. Happy V Day to you too! Are you off today?"

If there was anybody I would settle spending the day with, it was him.

Text Number Three was from my oldest daughter who was off at college. I loved her for how she always thought of me.

"Hey, babe. Mommy loves you, too and you have a good day," I messaged her.

And last there was "Mr. Cheater."

"GM, Happy Sweetheart Day, Sweetheart. I Love You!"

How could something as simple as a "Good Morning" text and an "I Love You," make everything alright in my world? I knew I would much rather have rolled over to him this morning instead of a text, or at least a message that promised plans for later today to give me something to look forward to.

He did think of me as soon as he got up. I know he really wants to be here, regardless of where he is.

The lies we tell ourselves.

The truth was I couldn't shake loose from this man. We had so many ties, including the financial support that he willingly gave when my marriage dissolved. He put my girls and me in our house, and made sure we had everything in it that we needed. When my divorce took me down a really rough road, he really had my back.

It did come at a cost.

He was constantly sneaking around and lying, especially to his wife. The time and money that he gave to me was all a secret from her. The way he saw it, even if his wife knew about his cheating, she wouldn't leave. She was dependent on him as I was, and, besides, she would never tarnish their precious family image with a divorce.

I must say though, he was one bad mofo and his money was

pretty long. Lord knows I wanted out of everything—the house, the relationship, the lies. His wife probably did too. Still we stayed. Each for our own reasons, but both of us holding onto our version of a fantasy of what could and should be. Whether or not either of us would ever choose to go remained to be seen. For today, I responded to his text and focused on the pieces of him that I had as opposed to those I didn't.

"GM and I love you too," I said simply.

That night turned out to be one of the craziest that I'd experienced in a long time. It was a movie that I could not have written myself. Absolutely crazy! I'd talked to my girl, Sasha, before all of the mess unfolded, but it would be months later before we caught up. I called to fill her in on everything that happened since.

"Umm, hello to you too, Sis!" I joked when she answered. "Tell me this. Am I going to have to take a trip to Dallas in order to talk to you? 'Cause please don't get me wrong because I will do just that, ma'am!"

She laughed out loud. "Wait a minute! I know we haven't talked, but I can explain. You know my hubby has been in transition with the new church where he will be the new musician at and then the job sent me out of town for the training in Arizona.

Nicole, you must have forgot. You know dang gone well I would have been talked to you by now girl!" she said excitingly.

"Okay, now I do remember you telling me you would be out of town for work and you would not be available during that time. My bad, Sis. Girl you know life falls apart when we don't talk for more than a day or two."

"So, okay, calm down and catch me up. My husband has got his music lesson students this evening so I am all ears. What's up, how the heck was your Valentine's Day?"

"Girl, I done been in all kind of drama wit' all the boos!"

"Whattttt!"

"Yeah, Sis. 'Mr. Cheater' came over here Valentine's Day night to surprise me with wine and roses and hunny I was walking out the door with 'Mr. Can't Get Right.' He took me to dinner that night and bought me a gift, but then 'Mr. Cheater' didn't say anything about it the next day. He talked to me and everything like things were good.

Then the night after V-Day I ended up leaving home and going to spend the night with 'Mr. Railroad' at the hotel because he was working a double. I don't know if you remember when he works long hours like that his job comps him a company hotel room. Well anyway, hunny, yo' boy came by here again. Baby, he said at about 6 am and my car was gone. He was all mad and shit, yelling at me talking about, 'Who you seeing? And don't lie about it. Babbbby I was shaking like booty meat."

"Oooh! Girl!" Sasha chimed in.

"Sis, I was too scared because I didn't know how much he knew. I was looking hella crazy while he was standing in this damn house starring me down."

"NOOOOO, Nicole, are you serious! You cannot have got into this much craziness like that since we last talked."

"Yes, ma'am, I did. Girl, 'Mr. Can't Get Right' found out about 'Mr. Cheater.' I told him I still wanted to kick it with both of them and his stupid self gon' say, 'Nicole, you strong as hell if you think I'm going to go along with that bullshit.'

I told him like this, would you prefer I lie to you? Of course he said, 'Hell nawl!' Then I looked at his ass and said, 'If you can't do it and you gotta let it go with me, then I understand.'"

She screamed into the phone. "Nicole! You are off the chain dog. You know you crazy, right?"

"What? Girl, you know he ain't worth me losing "Mr. Cheater" or "Mr. Railroad." Shit he can't do nothing for me but lick this cliq, trust and believe. Oh, he does that well, but he can keep the rest of him. Oh and he can fill my pockets with them Benjamins with his jailbird ass. I really don't even know how he lasted this long with me," I said as I busted out laughing.

"Nicole, you been said he low budget on your scale."

"He was though because he lie so much. He always got some drama with that silly baby momma or ex chic or whatever and he done been to jail."

"Girl, we all knew he didn't have much coming. Poor Lil' Can't Get Right! So what happened with the conversation about Railroad with my boy?"

"Well, actually, he is assuming Can't Get Right and Railroad are the same person, and, hunny, I was not going to tell him anything different. So I just told him I was talking to Railroad and that's where I had been. It was a mess too, Sis. He was acting all insecure about it all. Talking 'bout 'let me see a picture of him and where he work?' Now tell me why the hell would you want to see a damn picture?"

"So did you show him a picture of him, Nicole?"

"Girl, yes!"

"OMG, this is way too much! Just way too much. I can't even believe this, Nicole," she squealed.

"So you know being me, I had to show him the sexiest picture I had in my phone don't you? Truth be told if it really came down to it, I would be with Railroad and leave Cheater all the way alone. The only thing is, Railroad be pulling to many Houdini disappearing acts for me. I know most times he be at work because you know my crazy butt be driving over there to his job to see if his truck be there. He got me straight trippin'."

"Nicole, I cannot believe all this has happened. So Cheater done dealing with you?"

"Hell no!" I said so proudly, with a smile on my face. "He says to me, 'Do you love him? Because it's clear to me that you like him a hell of a lot to have him over here in this damn house I got you in.'

Just know this, friend. I'm still dealing with all they asses and Cheater just left here. He bought me lunch," I said arrogantly with a grin on my face.

"What are you gonna do, Nicole? You cannot keep this up for real though."

"Well, Sis. I really wanna be with Railroad, like all jokes aside. He talking about he been looking for an apartment in St. Louis so he can be closer to me and he wants something long term with me. He's been asking me about me living in this house and would I want to move into another house if we got together on that type of level. Clearly I said, 'No.' I'm not staying in this house. He went on to say, we would be able to use his military benefits to buy a house. Sis, I really like how we are not rushing, but that's where I stand on it though. He's who I want to be with."

I'd thought about where my heart was a lot since the whole Valentine's Day situation happened. That forced to me take a look at all of these men and these relationships for what they were.

I loved Mr. Cheater. But I'm also in love with what he provided me. If we removed the money he gave me from the equation, there wouldn't be enough there to hold us together, not while he was married. But I was stuck to him in a way that I didn't know how to undo.

"Well if that is what you wanna do, Nicole, then what's stopping you?"

"You already know the answer to that. You already know Mr. Cheater is paying off this debt on my credit from that damn divorce and helping me build it back up. I've got this bank account he opened in my name that he can have access to, so he can go make regular deposits for the credit cards, the house needs, and for me. I need that right now, sis. I'm trying to take care of this stuff, so I need him. I can't do it by myself."

"Okay, if you say so. But just know you can do it on your own."

"Sis, no, I can't." I know I sounded defensive. I was. If I felt like I could do without him, I would. "You know I am not getting any help from baby girl's dad and I have my college baby away at school. I need him right now!" I tried to convince her, but for real, I was trying to convince myself more than anything.

Let me call you back, hubby coming in," she said as she hurried off the phone.

"Okay, cool, we'll talk later."

It was one of those days when I had to just talk all this shit out and get it off my chest. So I dialed my friend, Linda, who I knew I could count on to hear me out.

"Hey Boo, what's up? Are you busy?" I asked when she picked up.

"Hey, Nicole. Nawl, girl, I'm not busy, just cutting."

"Oh, you're at the shop cutting a client?"

"Yeah, but it's a regular and I'm finishing up now. What's up with you?"

I sighed. "Girl, everything."

She picked up on the worry in my voice right away. "Oh lawd, let me let my client out the door. Hold on."

I sighed heavily again as I waited for her to come back to the phone.

"Okay, Nicole, lay it on me. What's going on with you,

girl?"

"Well I'm back feeling like I did before. I want to cut it off with Cheater and see what will happen with Railroad."

"Okay, soooooo, what's wrong with doing that?"

"You know I'm in this house and he is helping me fix my credit right now."

"Oh yeah." I appreciated that she could feel me on that. "But if being with Railroad would allow you to have a real relationship with your own man and that's what you want, then you have to weigh what's more important. Your credit or your heart, friend. But I do understand and you actually do love Cheater."

"Right, I'm just tired of feeling trapped in this," I said sadly.

"Nicole don't sound so sad, friend. Let me ask you this. Since you want to make it work with Railroad, are you sure that he is ready? 'Cause he still seems a bit flaky. Not answering his phone and you not seeing him for days at a time right after ya'll kick it. Do you think that's a good move for real? Have you thought it all the way through?"

I held the phone. She was right. About everything.

"Look, you my girl and whatever makes you happy I

support you. But I just don't want you to be super hurt if it don't work like you thought it would. Then another thing, what are you going to do with Can't Get Right or have you stop dealing with him already?"

"He still around, but not really. You already know he is not really in this equation of decisions, he just something to do right now."

She laughed out loud. "Girl! Yo' butt!"

"What? It's the truth. But you're right. I need to decide and stop flipping back and forth."

"Umm hmm. Well, look, my next client just walked in, so let me get back with you later. But, Nicole if how you're moving is bothering you, then you must do something different, my friend."

"You're right, but I'm good. It will be fine. I'll catch you later, Boo."

I hung up and sat there thinking about the mess I was in. I was caught in a mixed-up mess, dealing with three men at the same time and every one of them serves a different purpose. I was connected to Cheater based on his ability to provide for me financially. After all that he'd done for me, and continued to do, I felt like I owed him my loyalty. He'd proven time and time again that he would be there for me, and there was never a limit with him when it came to me, at least with his money. Despite all that he'd given me, the shame of it all, the sex, lies, secrets, and loneliness, haunted me every day. You wanna know why? It's because I'd just divorced a lying, cheating, dishonest man who was doing to me what Mr. Cheater was doing with me. I couldn't shake that guilt, no matter how hard I tried.

With Mr. Can't Get Right, hell, he was really something to do. If no one else was available, then he always was. He was my fallback. My safety net. When he was around, I didn't have to be alone. And he wanted me so bad that he would deal with whatever from me. I saw that as weakness and I could never commit to a man who I didn't respect in that way. But since I wasn't in love with him and I knew I had other options, it didn't matter. If he was there, cool. If he wasn't, so what.

I knew I was wrong. But, hey, I am just being real.

That leads me to Mr. Railroad who was an absolute catch. Well, at least that's what I tell myself. Even though I know he was totally playing me and controlling the flow of how we deal with one another. Now don't get me wrong, he was a great guy, on the surface at least. He was attractive, had an awesome job, his own place, and only one child that was about to graduate from high school and lived in another state, so not too much was required of him with that. We had great chemistry, and the sex was amazing with a capital "A."

I guess you're saying, 'Well, what's the damn problem then, Nicole?'

Let me give you a little more backstory to answer that. When I met him, he had a girlfriend that he was ending it with. She ended up moving out. Now it sounded like to me that they just didn't work out, but I can't deny that he seems to be a commitment phobe. I am constantly bringing up the same issues to him. The disappearing acts. The inconsistency. The not being available, emotionally or otherwise. I know he's full of shit! He knew that he was playing me, teasing me, stringing me along. He was a master at giving me just enough of what a relationship could be and making me want that more and more, only to never give it to me.

I'd been the side chick for way too long to somebody else's husband. Really, to every one of these men. As I sat there with my bottle of wine, supposedly sorting it all out and coming up with a conclusion in my mind, I had nothing figured out as far as what I was going to do. Actually, that wasn't true. I did know what I was planning to do.

Pour myself another glass and keep playing the game until the game was up.

The Naked Truth

The truth was I thought my problem was in dealing with all of these men. But the reality was that I was dealing with each of them because I refused to deal with the one person who was at the root of it all—me. That would come in time. (I hope you'll stay with me in these pages until I get there.)

There comes a time when we have to just get by ourselves, look at things exactly the way they are, and figure out why we are making the choices we do. We have to find the courage to see ourselves for who and what we are. Dig down in the cracks looking. And the part we've played in our own headaches and heartaches. Once we get to the bottom of our mess, we can see it all. Then we have to accept it for what it is deciding to never be there again. Hopefully. You see, sometimes acceptance doesn't always lead to change right away. They say old habits are hard to break. Seeing yourself for less than what you are is a deep, deep wound that won't heal overnight, and neither will filling that wound with people and things that can never make you happy. Even you after you see yourself and the decisions you've made for what they are, even when you know you need to operate and choose differently, you may still continue to operate in a pattern of bad choices until the end finally comes.

And when it does, remember where we are is no one's fault but our own.

In the end, remember who is to blame.

"For I know that good itself does not dwell in me, that is, in my sinful nature. For I have the desire to do what is good, but I cannot carry it out. For I do not do the good I want to do, but the evil I do not want to do—this I keep on doing."

Romans 7:18-19 (NIV)

7

SURRENDING ALL

Iwas in my bathroom, jamming, listening to my dope playlist. I was getting myself fly, dressing to go out for the evening. I looked good, hunny! I am talking about sexy. And I felt sexy too.

"Hate on me Haters, now or later, 'cause I'm gonna do me, you'll be mad baby!!!" I sang along with Jill Scott at the top of my lungs. I was putting the finishing touches on my lipstick when I caught a real look at myself in the mirror. I stopped and put the tube down on the countertop.

"Why are you doing this, Nicole?" I asked myself as I stood there staring at my reflection. "What are you saying about yourself, dealing with three emotionally unavailable men at the same damn time?"

I sat down on the side of my tub with my elbows pressed into the top of my knees. I knew it was something on the inside of me that kept attracting men that were no good for my life. I finally realized something that night. I was looking good, smelling good, and about to hit the club and later hook up with one of the lucky three. I was covering it all up with the makeup, sexy dress, and expensive perfume. I was covering up the woman who kept attracting men that belonged to other women, men who were liars, because I was a fraud and was deceptive myself.

It was easy (yes I said easy) for me to deal with men with a woman or a wife or who would lie to me since that's what I expected. I felt like all men in my life would eventually cheat or leave. So I just decided I would beat them to the punch or save myself the heartache.

I only wanted men who were already obligated so I didn't have to accept the insecurities about myself. I figured I could have the benefits and the company of a man, without ever having to face the truth. His or my own.

Isn't that what we do? Hide from the truth? They're not all ours anyway, right? So we convince ourselves that we don't have to have him all of the time. Or when we're feeling extra, if he was available, we wouldn't want him anyway. He doesn't have to respect or love us. We can settle for the simple things like money, sex, and a few dinners and texts here and there. It was okay. It was enough? Wasn't it?

This thinking was so much bigger than these men. It was about me, and all the things I feared most. At the top of that list was not having a loyal, trustworthy, and honest man. I'd never seen what that looked like, starting with my own father. I never had the love or acceptance from what should have been my first love, my daddy.

It hit me while sitting in my bathroom on the side of my tub. I had not yet faced my own insecurities of truth about the pain of my past, the abandonment by my father, the divorce, and my serious trust issues. I walked out of my bathroom, picked up my cell phone, and sent a group text to my girlfriends to let them know I would catch them later and I was staying in because I was tired. That was a big lie. I just needed time to think. Alone.

As I started to undress, thinking about the emotional and mental mess I'd created of my life, the tears came. But these were tears that I'd never cried before. They were painful tears, the tears that come from the very depths of my soul. The tears that come when you finally see your truth for what it really is. And it hurts.

For the first time, I thought about what I was doing and how I had been living my life. And it was scary. I got in bed, my tears soaking my pillow as I sobbed, I decided that I'd had better face my ugly, trifling self and the internal issues that I had or accept living a lie.

I needed to talk to somebody. I tried to pull myself together as I dialed my sister-friend, Sasha, who lived in Dallas, Texas. When she answered, I tried to make small talk. But she knew better. We'd always had some keen sense of energy and could feel when something was wrong with the other.

She stopped my rambling. "Nicole what's wrong with you?"

I kept faking it. "You know what, I'm coming to the Big D.

I'm coming to Dallas to see you!" I said excitedly as if nothing was wrong.

"Yeah right! Nicole, whatever!"

"No, seriously. I'm getting on a plane and I'm coming to see my friend. I'm looking at my calendar right now and I've got these dates between November 12th and November 17th available because I'll be on vacation for two weeks. I'm going to call you back tomorrow after I look at the flights and pick what days would be best."

"Sis, you are for real aren't you?"

"Like a heart attack." I assured her that I would call her the next day to firm up plans and we said goodnight before hanging up.

I woke up the next morning, scared senseless and soaking wet with sweat. I'd had one of the most terrifying dreams I had ever remembered having. I jumped out of my bed and ran to the bathroom mirror. For some reason, I needed to see my face. I needed to see what I looked like. As I stood there, I thought about what I had just dreamed about and an overwhelming feeling came over me, the kind of feeling you get when you've been seen doing something wrong by one of the mothers at the church. You know, that crazy, shameful feeling of guilt.

I had to get to Dallas as soon as possible.

I grabbed my computer, got online, and looked at my flight options. I booked and called my friend to let her know that I was coming for sure.

She screamed with excitement and started planning our itinerary. "Okay, let's make plans. What do you want to do when you get here? You wanna go out? You wanna shop? What's the plan? Oh my gosh, I'm super geeked you're actually coming, Sis!"

I'd been looking forward to seeing her for so long, and finally getting to do all of the things that she mentioned. But this time, I really just wanted to get away from my drama, spend time with my girl, and piece my mind back together as much as I could in a few days.

"You know what? I don't wanna go out and shopping is not really on my list either. I just want us to have some friend time and I wanna come down to kind of clear my head a little bit. I do want to go to some good eateries, places we don't have here in St. Louis."

She understood, like I knew she would. "Okay, I got you. We can definitely do that."

"You know, Sister, I do have one request. I want to visit the Potter's House Church, if it is not too far from where you live and the hotel I will be staying at. Do you know the one I'm talking about? Have you been there?"

She told me that the church was about an hour away from

where she was, but if I wanted to go we would make it happen. So there the trip was set and everything was in place. I couldn't wait. But of course you know it couldn't be that easy, right?

Excited about the trip, I called my "main" man-friend, Mr. Cheater, to tell him.

"Hey, you. What's up? I said sweetly when he picked up. "Hey, nothing much. What's going on with you, baby?" "Well I just got off the phone with my girlfriend in Dallas and I am going down to see her in about a week. My flight leaves on the 13th at 3:35 pm. Do you think you can take me to the airport?"

"Hmm. Trip to Dallas...," he said, with the most suspicious tone of voice, as if it was something I wasn't telling him about my quickly planned trip. "This is all of a sudden, Nicole. You haven't said anything about this before now."

"Yeah, I know. I figured I will be on vacation for two weeks and it would be a good time to go see her because she has some time off as well."

I could tell from his silence that he wasn't going to let it go. He wasn't happy at all about me being away and not accessible, even if it was for a short time. He probably didn't realize it, but he was wearing his insecurities on his sleeve.

When he dropped me off at the airport a week later, the air was thick with attitude.

As we pulled into the drop off location in front of my terminal,

I felt his heat, but I refused to acknowledge it.

I really didn't give a damn. I knew the only reason he was suspicious was because he'd found out about Mr. Railroad recently, and was probably thinking I was going to be traveling with him. We all know that was a lie. I needed and deserved this trip to get away from all the madness that had been going on in my life. It was time for me to unplug for real and I couldn't care less what he was feeling. I knew why I was leaving and who did he think he was to even be mad?

DUDE YOU HAVE A WIFE AT HOME! I thought to myself as I got out of the car. I refused to allow him and his BS ruin my energy or this trip.

After pulling my bags from the trunk, he sarcastically told me to have a safe and fun trip, gave me a half ass kiss, and we said our goodbyes. I walked away looking super fly and sexy in my black and light gray athlete gear with my big ole' booty looking ever so round in those fitted sweatpants. I was getting hungry looks from the baggage claim guys outside who check the bags in for the flights. I knew Mr. Cheater was still watching my every move, so I turned and looked back at him. Sure enough, he was still sitting in the car, with that angry, jealous look on his face. Maybe he sensed that the Nicole who was leaving would not be the Nicole who came back. I was planning to return from Dallas as a different, damn woman.

As I boarded the plane, I felt a sense of urgency and calm all at the same time. It seemed my soul knew something was about to happen, something that would change the direction of my thoughts, my actions, and my understanding in the days to come.

My flight to Texas arrived on time and I was ready to see my sister-friend! I exited the plane and headed to the baggage claim to retrieve my luggage and, while doing so, I called her to let her know I had landed and to find out where she wanted to pick me up from. I got her voicemail, so I left a message and continued down to the luggage claim area.

Standing there waiting for my bag to pop out onto the round-a-bout, I called again. The phone rang a few times, and the voicemail picked up again. "Hey, girl. I've touched down in the Big D!"

I was starting to get a little worried as I rolled my luggage over near an outside window, hoping I would just happen to see her pulling up outside or even already waiting for me. I stared out of the window, but my friend was nowhere in sight. I checked my phone for the time to see if the flight had arrived a bit early and maybe she just hadn't arrived yet, but I'd arrived right on time. I grew more anxious by the second. This was not like her at all.

I kept an eye out for her car from the window, and kept calling her phone. The third time, the call went straight to voicemail. Now I am really freaking out. I had no other way to reach her and, all of a sudden, the sky was dark. Within minutes, it was a full-blown storm and pouring rain. The wind was blowing and trees swaying from left to right. I couldn't help but think about the clothes I had packed for my trip as I watched the temperature on the digital signs in the airport drop. When I checked the weather forecast for the few days I would be there, it was supposed to be in the mid-seventies. Now this wicked storm had ushered out the heat and bought the air down to the fifties. This trip was not starting out like I planned. At all.

At least five more unanswered calls to my friend and forty-five minutes later, I decide that I needed to just grab a taxi to my hotel. As I am walking towards the exit to find one, my phone rings with an unknown number.

Needless to say, I was not in the mood for any more surprises.

> "Hello!" I answer with all of the heat that was boiling to my surface.

> "Oh My God, sister. It's me! Have you arrived?" My friend was frantic on the other end of the phone.

> "Girl, yes! I am here!" I started to feel all of my attitude melt away.

"I'm on my way. My phone died and there was a very bad accident on the route to the airport, so that's why I'm so late getting there. I am using the cell phone of a very nice man because I explained to him that you have been at the airport over an hour waiting on me and this was your first time coming here and to please let me use his phone but never mind I will see you in about 25 minutes sis. I'll pick you up near the rental car area of baggage claims, see you soon. Love ya!"

I don't know if she took a breath, but I was so happy to hear her voice that I just let her go. Smiling as I hung up the phone, I was so thankful that she was okay and on her way. I laughed to myself, hoping that this was not an indication of how my trip would be for the next four days!

I waited outside for a bit, and finally, my friend pulled up, jumps out of the car, and gave me the biggest hug ever.

I hugged her in return. "What the heck, sister? It has gotten super cold out here. What is going on? I'm seriously not prepared for this weather!" I threw my bags in the back and I jumped into her truck quickly. "I might need to go find me a coat because I don't have anything much thicker than a really lightweight leather jacket I brought."

"Girrrrllllll!" she laughed! "A coat in Texas? That will be a scavenger hunt, but, okay, after I take you to your hotel to check in, we can go see what we can find."

We pulled up to my hotel and I left her in the car to check in and drop off my luggage. When I got back to the truck, I noticed a frown on her face as she fumbled with the buttons on the console.

"What the heck! I think my heat just went out in here!"

"You are kidding."

"As soon as you got out and went in, it started to blow

cold air! Don't worry, we will be fine and we are still going to run by the store to find you a coat for sure."

We hit the stores, and while she was right about the horrible selection of coats, I finally found a cute, wool blend jacket that would be perfect for this drastic weather change. And even better, it was marked down on clearance.

"Thank you God! This trip was finally starting to look up!"

We were having the best time. My friend took me to some of the best eateries the city could offer, and I loved every minute of it. My girl made me feel so loved and at home. It was exactly what I needed.

Before I knew it, it was my last night in Dallas. That night, our girl time was like no other. She came to my hotel room to hang out and we just talked about everything under the sun. We chatted about where we were in our lives and, in the midst of that, I bought up my so-called relationship. I was completely honest with her about how it had been making me feel lately and how I was unable to break it off due to what I felt I was receiving from it.

She stopped me from talking and said, "Sister, when you are really ready to do something different you will. So for the time being, try giving it to God and leaving it there."

"To be honest, I'm not sure how but I feel like this trip, as spontaneous as it was, was made possible for a very specific reason and I'm almost afraid of that reason. I need to tell you something.

My friend looked back at me with her eyes wide. "What is it, Nicole?" She had apprehension in her voice, as if she was unsure about what was coming next.

I looked at her with misty eyes. "The day I called you and said I was coming down here, do you remember that day? "Yessssss…and?"

"Well after I got off the phone with you that night, before I went to bed, I got on my knees and began to pray about my life and what I had been doing with it and with who and that I needed a change. I told God that I really wanted it, but didn't know how on my own. Once I feel asleep that night, it was almost as if I was still awake. It was so strange, Sis.

I had a dream, and in my dream my ideal of the voice of God came to me and said if I continued on the road of life that I'm on, it would lead to a fall into what we believe hell looks like. It felt as real a child birth. And so that morning, I woke up, went online, and purchased my flight. I called you and told you I was coming. Now that I'm here, I think this trip was bigger than just wanting to see you and clear my head." I started to cry.

She just let me get it out. Through her own tears she said, "Well the time is now my friend!"

She hugged me and we said our goodbyes for the night. We'd

see each other in a few hours for our early morning drive to The Potter's House for church service. I started gathering my things to pack my bag and head back to St. Louis afterwards.

I woke up the next morning, a little sad as I got dressed. It was my last day in Dallas and the time with my girl was coming to an end. But I couldn't wait to get to the church. Neither of us had been there so it would be an experience for the both of us. She picked me up from my hotel that morning pretty early because it was going to take about an hour to get there. We chatted it up all the way there, and before I knew it we were waiting in a line of cars to pull into the parking lot.

Immediately, there was a sense of warmth when we walked inside. The building was huge, but you wouldn't think, from the way people moved and smiled around us, that this was a church pastored by such a famous person. It actually seemed like your normal place of worship, just on a larger scale.

We were greeted by smiling faces, but once we got in the door, we had no idea where to go. I stopped a gentleman who seemed to be a greeter standing at what I thought were the doors to the sanctuary.

"Excuse me, sir."

"Good morning, how can I help you?"

"This is our first time here, and we need a little direction on where the entrance to the sanctuary is."

He smiled. "Sure not a problem." He gestured for another member to take his place at the door where he was standing. Motioning for us to follow him, he gladly escorted us to a counter on another side and explained to the ladies there that it was our first time visiting. After assuring us that we'd be taken care of, he left us to head back to his post.

A friendly woman handed us each an information card to fill out. Once we'd completed those and gave them back to her, she offered us a gift bag with what appeared to be a few CDs inside. She pointed out an area that was just behind us where we could go and have some morning refreshments and have a seat. Service hadn't started yet, so we could either wait there or proceed into the sanctuary. When we told her that we'd rather go in and find a seat, she waved another member over to us.

> "Welcome to the Potter's House. We have a special section for first-time guests down near the front of the sanctuary, so please follow me."

As we walked in, the inside of the sanctuary was really nice and big, but not as large as it seemed on television.

We were seated in about the seventh row from the altar. I was super excited and couldn't wait to get a word from Bishop Jakes.

Soon the service began. Again, I was surprised that the praise and worship portion was just like every other church. There was nothing over the top, no super fancy lights and cameras. Just singers, instruments, and praise.

Nothing like what I thought. That just goes to show you to never judge a book by its cover or from the views of others. You have to venture inside for yourself to see what things are all about. We sang, danced, and clapped with the rest of the congregation, enjoying the music until the Bishop came to the stage.

When he got up and began to speak, he ushered in

the presence of the Lord and gave us a morning prayer. After our collective "Amen," I reached into my purse to pull out my IPad to take notes while he preached. I knew this would be a word that I wanted to remember.

>"Today's sermon is titled, 'This Is No Time To Lose Your Head."

My eyes shot up and I looked at him, and then I immediately locked eyes with my friend.

"Nicole, this can't be real," she said in disbelief.

I quickly realized this trip was to see my friend but it was ultimately the place God needed me to be in. God needed to separate me from my surroundings to get my full attention and for me to have a clear mind to hear what I needed for my future self. It hit me right then that I was exactly where I needed to be.

The prayer I prayed that night that God came for me was what brought me here. He was telling me to not lose my head. To not forget what He told me to do. To stay strong.

As the congregation stood for the reading of the Word, Bishop began teaching from the book of Ephesians, starting with Chapter 6, verse 17.

"Take the helmet of salvation and the sword of the Spirit, which is the word of God."

When I tell you my mind was blown in that moment! I felt the ever-present energy of God that morning during the entire service. As I prepared my offering envelope, my friend leaned over to me.

> "Nicole, do you know the elderly man next to me just handed me a fifty dollar bill and said God told him to bless me?" I looked down at her hand after she tapped my leg to show me the crisp fifty dollar bill. With the most overwhelming look on her face she whispered, "Oh My God!"

Bishop Jakes was coming to a close as the service came to an end. "The holy spirit is after something this morning. So for those of you who pressed your way to get here this morning with the bad weather, if you are someone whose mind has been under severe attack, if you have had to have a fake smile and you haven't been able to have a fresh clear mind for the Lord to anoint, rush your way to this altar."

Before he could get the rest of the words out of his mouth, I had closed my Bible app on my Ipad and was moving out into the aisle with tears streaming down my face. I hurried down to the front of the church. I knew right there, at the altar in a foreign new place, was where God needed me to be to hear the message he had for me. I came to Dallas not just to see my friend but to get my head back. I had to not lose my head so that God could save my life.

I closed my eyes and just allowed the spirit of God to wash over me as tears poured down my face. I cried tears of devastation as I thought about where I had allowed my life to go and the people I allowed myself to lie down with. I fell to my knees at the altar.

I recalled a lady's voice telling me, "Sweetheart, let it out. Whatever your pain is, let it out and give it to God!"

Right at that moment, I felt my body go limp and I found myself stretched out, belly and face to the floor just weeping, wailing, and crying out.

> "God heal me. I need you and I can't do this alone. I surrender, oh God, I surrender it all."

And there it was. The final piece of finally giving it all over to Him. I felt the spirit of grace in that moment. Standing over top of me, I heard Bishop Jakes speaking in tongues and saying, "God is going to restore you. Why do you think God brought you to Dallas? Your bad yoke will be broken."

I knew things were going to be okay then. I didn't know how exactly, but I trusted it to be so. As Bishop closed out the altar prayer and I began to slowly get up from the floor.

My friend was right there with me, her face fully wet from tears she hugged me. "All is well, sister, all is well now!" We both smiled, walked back to our seats, and prepared for the closing remarks. She was so right. All was well with my soul. I felt it.

When we got back to the car, we were warm with blessings and joy on the inside, but freezing from the cold temperature on the outside. As we waited for the car to warm up and the heat to start pumping, we sat there for what seemed like twenty minutes in total silence, not even looking over at one another, in awe of what had just happened.

After a few minutes, I turned, looked at her, and screamed, "I Got My Head Back, sister!"

"YESSSSSSSSSSSSSS!"

We fell out laughing as she drove off the parking lot. We grabbed some lunch and she drove me to the airport to catch my flight.

After I checked my luggage at the stand outside, she got out to hug me. "Before you leave this place, I must pray for you." She grabbed my hands tight, and prayed for my mental clarity and strength to handle what was to come, along with my safe return back to St. Louis. I left Dallas feeling renewed and with an assignment about my life.

The Naked Truth

Sometimes when things are happening in our lives, we can't see the forest for the trees. We're standing in the middle of it all. When we decide that something has to change in our lives, we often need to be in a different environment to receive clarity and direction for our next steps. Realizing that change needs to happen is the simple part, but actually making the change? Now that is where help is needed to lose the strongholds we struggle with. My struggle had me in the head lock and I needed a one-on-one God experience to realize His heart for me. All that was required was the will to change and that the change was mine to have. My time in Dallas reminded me of that.

If you need to hear from God, you may need to come out of your physical environment to do it. When God comes to change your life, He has to get your attention. He has to take you out of your mess so you can get the message. You may not need to hop on the next plane, but maybe you do. Maybe you need to go for a short trip or a long walk on a path that you've never seen before. Whatever you have to do, where ever you have to go, don't be afraid. Don't wait. This is your pass out of your pain.

The Lord has heard my cry for mercy; the Lord accepts my prayer. Psalms 6:9 (NIV)

NICOLE M. BENTLEY

8

PRIVATE PARTY

Lying in my bed alone, I glance over at my clock and see those blazin', red numbers that read 3:47 a.m. I pick up my phone and send a text to Mr. Railroad. "Hey you, are you working?"

Just like clockwork, he sends a fast response. He always seems to answer in the midnight hour.

> "Hey what's up. Just about to leave work in a second. What are you doing up?"

> "I can't sleep."
> "Oh, really. That's not good. Can I come see you?"
> "Sure. How long will it be before you get here?"
> "I'm leaving out now. I will see you in about 10 minutes."
> "Okay!"

I jump out of my bed and hurry to the bathroom. I quickly brush my teeth and took a baby wipe to my face to get a quick refresh. Then changed out of my mismatched pajamas into a much cuter set, my snug, vintage gray cotton short set, with Minnesota Twins written across the shirt. I knew these showed off my curves so perfectly but not showing everything, if you know what I mean. Another quick glance in the mirror and my phone buzzed with a message. He was pulling up. I write back that the door was unlocked.

Mr. Railroad walks in as I am back in bed, leisurely watching television.

"Hey, beautiful," he says as he walks over to my side of the bed. He leans in to give me a kiss, which I received happily. He took his jacket off and placed it on the chair in my room, and then sat to take off his shoes and sweater, which he laid neatly on the chair next to the bed.

"How was work?" I asked.

"Hectic! We had a train jump the track today. It wasn't too bad of an incident, but it made us pretty busy after that. Forget about work, how was your trip to see your friend?"

"Oh, my trip was great. She was happy to see me. We did a lot of girl talk and catching up. And she took me to some great food places. You know restaurants that's not here at home."

"That sounds like a good trip. New food is always

good."

I enjoyed talking to him most of the time, but there was something in me that wanted more than our usual small talk. I'd been in deep thinking mode since I came back from Dallas, and beating around the bush with these men was no longer on the menu.

"Hey, I need to ask you something," I said.
"Sure, what do you want to ask?"

"Tell me, what we are doing? What is this that we have?" He looked puzzled. "What we have?"

"Yes, I mean, I seem to only see you late nights after work, or we may go out somewhere together every once in a while, but, I mean, really nothing more than that. I understand the situation with your ex and that she has moved out and that's over, but who am I to you? Just your friend, your lady, your lover? What is the deal?" I said firmly.

He sits up, clears his throat, and leans closer to me. He looks into my eyes, and softly strokes my cheek. "You are all of the above, Nicole. I thought you knew that."

"Umm, how would I know that? You have never formally

stated I was your lady. It seems we keep doing this cute cat and mouse thing. I see you, we have amazing sex then I don't see or hear from you for several days. I don't know what you are used to but that doesn't work for me. I need something more consistent. Like really. How are you okay with us like that and you sit and say you love me?"

I waited for a split second before continuing my rant. "What do you love? You barely know me because you're always missing in action. I mean, look, I am a realist and I really do like you. Hell, I feel like I'm falling in love with you. But shit, tell me if this is just a fuck thing for you and I will choose how I will deal with this from there."

"Why would you say that, Nicole? No this is not a sex thing, it's more than that. I am with you. You are with me."

I'd heard this before. Too many times. "How?"

"We are in a relationship, baby."

"Oh really? When were you going to tell me that? If I need to say this to you then, if we are in a 'relationship'," I yelled, while using both of my hands to gesture air quotes, "I need to let you know this. From here on out, since you have clarified our relationship, the next time you leave me and I don't talk to you for days at a time or I don't see you and when I do there is no excusable reason like work or death, I will not have anything to say. This will just be over. You just don't do that to someone. I understand people need self-time and you are implying to me there is nothing else going on. But to not respond to a text message or even answer when I call is total bullshit and I'm not doing it anymore. So you let me know right now if that is something you can do and if not. I understand and will move on 'cause I'm not going to deal with it."

"I'm sorry for making you feel like that and I understand. I'll do better," he said as he grabs me and pulls me close.

For some reason as the words were coming out of his mouth, I felt like that spell I had been under from his good looks, amazing body, and willingness to see me in the late hours no longer worked for me. I wanted someone for me, all of the time, not just these late-night booty calls that clearly I was so willing to give.

I expected that after I finished all of my fussing and we kissed and made up, that he would try to get what he came for. I had no desire to be with him, and I guess our conversation killed his mood. He didn't even try to get close to me. It was clearly not a get-laid-kind of night for either of us. The truth has a way of doing that to you.

"Well since we got a much-needed conversation out of the way, I'm sure you are tired from being at work," I said. "So get you some rest."

He laid next to me and we both drifted off to sleep as the sun rose.

I woke up feeling so much better after speaking my heart and mind to him. I looked over, and Mr. Railroad was still very much asleep. I was prepared to just lay there and look at him for a second when my house phone rang loudly. I grabbed the cordless next to my bed, and the Caller ID screen read, "Private Caller."

Oh shit! I thought to myself.

It was Mr. Cheater. The clock read 1:13 pm, which meant he had probably been calling for his usual stop by and lunch with me, but when I didn't answer my cell as usual,
he decided to call the house phone which he really never does.

I damn sure couldn't pick up with Mr. Railroad in my bed, that's for sure. I threw the cover off of me and rush to the living room window to peep out the blinds and make sure his black car wasn't parked outside in the driveway.
I really need to stop this shit, sneaking and creeping.

Aside from this whole scenario just getting old, I knew Cheater would lose his mind if he knew I had regular late night visits in the house he put me in. I had to think fast and get this dude out of my bed and out of this house before things got ugly.

Let me act like I have somewhere to be.

I strolled back into the bedroom. Railroad was starting to stir. "Hey sleepyhead," I said softly. "I hate to do this to you, but I need to get dressed and go pick my daughter up from her Dad's. So you're gonna have to get up because she is coming back home with me."
"Oh, it's cool, I understand." He gets up, grabs his clothes, and walks into the bathroom.

Now, Nicole you are playing way too much, I thought to myself. Having him in this house and knowing that Mr. Cheater has a damn key, even if he has never used it, I was playing with fire. Just my luck today was the day he decided to come in there. Now I had to think of a good enough lie to explain why I wasn't answering my phone all morning. I knew he would ask when I talked to him.

As I stood by the bed crafting my tale, Railroad comes out of the bathroom. I quickly move him towards the front door, and after a goodbye peck on the lips, I close it behind him.

Then I dart down the hall back to my bedroom to make my bed up and spray some Gain-scented Febreeze to get the unmistakable scent of Railroad's fresh cologne and sweet Black and Mild cigars out of the air and sheets. I grabbed my purse and left the house. I jumped in the car and headed towards the highway.

As I took the exit, I nearly jumped out of the seat when my phone rang. Thankfully it was only Can't Get Right. I did not have time for him at the moment. I let the call go to voicemail as I released a sigh of relief and just drove. I had no idea where I was going, but I didn't care as long as the destination was anywhere but my house.

I decided to visit my friend at her barbershop, hoping that she could be my alibi for why I was unavailable for Mr. Cheater's phone calls. As I pull up to the shop, I notice there are no cars.

Dammit, Nicole! It's Monday and the shop is closed.
Well I might as well get in front of this conversation with Mr. Cheater and go ahead and call him.

As I dialed the number, I tried to shake the nervousness inside of me so it wouldn't come out in my tone of voice.

He didn't let me get a word out. "Where have you been?"
Before I could respond, he barked again. "Someone just walked into my office, I will call you back."

I sadly hung up the phone. I knew he was pissed off, and considering he wasn't trusting me very much right now after the whole Valentine's Day fiasco and how I was busted, who knows what he was thinking.

Oh well, whatever. I couldn't allow myself to wallow in it. I just had to wait until he called back. I turned around to go back home and wait for the stormy argument with him.

While on the road, I decided to call right back.

"Hey baby, where you at?"

"On my way home," I responded, slightly annoyed. "What's up?"

"I just wanted to explain the little situation with my ex getting your phone number, Nicole—"

I stopped him.

"You know what, you don't have to explain anything because you lie so much I ain't gonna believe nothing coming out of your mouth."

He was referring to an out-of-the-blue call that I got from this chick a few days ago. I couldn't believe that a grown woman would actually call another grown woman on some bullshit about why she was supposedly sleeping with her man. If she had to call and ask, she already knew the answer. But I wasn't going to entertain her or him anymore. I was done.

"To be honest with you, I wasn't even going to mention the silly girl calling me and playing. The conversation she recorded about how you feel about me and me not meaning anything to you. You know what, I'm done with this and you 'cause I really don't have time for no damn games. I thought, if nothing else, if I was always honest with you, you would be honest with me, but I see you are not that kind of man. You still playing games. So you go ahead and be with yo girl because it's clear she is silly too, so you two deserve each other."

"Nicole, baby, don't do this," he pleaded as his game flashed before his eyes. "I want you in my life you make me a better man. I've been trying to let her know I'm with you, but she stalking me."

"Well that's your problem and no longer mine. I was honest with you about me being with ol' boy and him getting me my house I'm in and how that whole relationship and me staying with him was because I wanted to see what was up with you first. But as I can see, I may as well stay in this bullshit I'm in with him. At least I'm getting something from it because this what you have going on and the drama you bring. I'm not about that. At all."

"Nicole, don't do this. Please, baby."

"I'm done, straight up. So if you would please just not call me anymore. BYE!" I hung up the phone thinking, one down.

The phone buzzed with text messages. While waiting at the red stop light, I read.
"Nicole baby I Love You don't do this baby please."

I rolled my eyes and put the phone back in my purse. Getting rid of him gave me a bit of relief. Pulling up in my driveway, I felt like I totally needed a nap. I walked in, figuring I would do some laundry.

I drop my purse and keys on the kitchen table and go down to the basement to sort my clothes and I hear a knock on the back door. The unexpected sound scared me. No one would know I was downstairs, so there was no reason to not come to the front door. I quietly walk up the basement steps to the living room to look outside. Mr. Cheater's black car was parked in the driveway.

Oh crap! He was supposed to call me back. Oh well, here we go!

I stalled to pull my nerves together. "Who is it?"

"It's me, Nicole. Open the door."

"Oh," I said, pretending that I didn't know. I unlocked the door, and before I could get it fully opened, he pushes it and storms past me. He sat his keys down on the kitchen table and walked directly back to my bedroom. Knowing that I needed to play it cool, I went back downstairs to finish sorting my laundry. I hear him yell for me.

"Nicole! Nicole!"

I come up the stairs and realize he is still in my bedroom. I walk in to find him sitting in the chair in the corner of my room.

"Nicole, do you love him?" His question is completely out of nowhere.

I looked startled. "Love who?" My heart was practically beating out of my chest.

"Nicole, let's not do this," he said calmly. "Do you love him? The guy you've been with and please don't insult me like I'm crazy because I know that I'm not.

"At first you were just responding to my messages later than you used to, then all of a sudden you are always going out with your friends and staying out all night long—"

Now, I was starting to get pissed. How dare he question me? Did he forget that he had a whole wife at home?

"Umm, wait, let me stop you. Since when did I get a curfew and when and where does it say I can't stay out all night with my friends? The last time I checked, I am a grown woman."

"Yeah, you are grown and, no, you don't have a curfew, Nicole. But you being out all night and not responding to my messages, I get worried."

"Well maybe if you were here full time you wouldn't have to worry and I wouldn't have to check in and out like I'm a kid. You get all trippy on me because I don't answer my phone or text you right back. I don't see what the problem is because clearly you get to come over here whenever you choose so what is the problem."

"You seem to have everything you want, so why are you complaining?"

"You know what? I can't do this anymore."

"Do what Nicole?"
"This!" I lifted my hands in the air. "Us! I can't do this,

I said angrily."

"What is it that you want, Nicole?"

"I don't want anything. This isn't about you getting me anything. This is about me being done. I want you to leave and this is over."

"Are you serious?" He had a smirk on this face but I knew he didn't think any of this was funny. "Nicole, if I leave, I'm not coming back." His voice was stern and sure.

"You know what, I just can't do this anymore. I don't care where you go, I just want you to leave here. You can go be with somebody else who can take my place in this mess, or better yet, you know what? Maybe you need to go home to your wife and figure out why you are sleeping with me. You are giving me everything I want and not fixing what's broken over there with her. You keep sleeping around on her and for God knows how long, even before me..."

He stood up, looked at me, and moved towards the bedroom door. "Nicole, what is it? Do you want to see this guy on a regular basis? Fine, I understand you deserve your own man. Let's talk about this. Let's talk through it."

"I don't think there is anything I need to talk through."
As he shook his head and kept walking, I hurried to the
door. "Oh, and so we are clear about me being done, I
will be moving out of the house also."

He swung back around. "Wait, what? Moving? Why are
you leaving the house, Nicole? I have completely began
remodeling this house for you. The kitchen is done,
bathroom is done for you, just like you wanted. I mean
a total gut job on this house for you. You were just
getting estimates to finish the basement and add
another bathroom. This house is yours, what am I
going to do with it?"

"I don't know and I don't care. Sell it, rent it! It's not
my concern. I will be looking for a new place. I will try
to give you a notice as soon as I can, but I'm done. Can
you just leave?" I felt like he was sucking all of the air
of the room. I needed him gone.

"Nicole, if I leave here, I'm not coming back and there
is nothing left to say," he warned me again. " If you
want to sit and talk about what's going on with you and
you want something else, we can talk about it."

"No, I'm fine."
"So you really want me to leave and you're done?"

"Yes!"

The hurt on his face was real. He slowly walked to the door and stopped one last time. "Just tell me why. Can you tell me that?"

"It's what I want."

"Why now though, Nicole?"

"I deserve more than this and I deserve someone who is willing to do that and if not, I'll be by myself.

"I do that though, Nicole."

"Yeah, but I don't want it on your terms, with your wife. I want all of a man not just a piece of him with his money attached," I said. "Baby, let's talk."

"No, just leave. Please."

"Nicole, if I go I'm not coming back." He said for what I knew was the last time, unlocking the door and opening it.

I said nothing. And he was gone.

"Okay," I said to the empty house. I locked the door to my house and my heart as far as he was concerned.

I stood there so sad, but yet proud and thankful for the power I had in that moment. I allowed my soul to have a little party for my heart. I knew the time had come to press forward into what was for me. I was so happy that I finally ended that selfish relationship. Where we both had been serving ourselves, and it was wrong.

Taking my life back sent me into a mental praise and the tears began to flow from my eyes. My body trembled from so many emotions, but surprisingly the most prevalent feeling was strength. I knew if I wanted more for myself, I had to be willing to give up more. I trusted the experience I had in Dallas to be real and true for my life, and I also remembered the dream of what my future looked like if I kept living the way I was living. I decided I was going to trust that, as much as this hurt, there was something else waiting for me on the other side of this pain. There was something really good out there for me, and I could never have it standing neck deep in deception, adultery, and fornication. All of that was killing my future, and it was time for me to follow my heart, and learn who I really was and what I really wanted. I had to stop running from the woman I was so I could become the woman I wanted to be. For me to get what was for me, I had to spend some quality time with myself, get my head back in this game of self love, and devote my energy to myself and cleansing my hard places, the places I ignored that had me bound to the ugliness of my true self.

I walked into my bathroom and looked at myself in the mirror, with ugly flowing tears soaking my face and sobbing.

"Nicole, you are a hoe, you are selfish, you are a user, you are insecure…" I started to break myself down so I or no one else could ever do it again. "You are needy, you are searching for love, you are divorced and a two-time single mother. You look beautiful, but you are a total mess on the inside." I sobbed as I faced the ugliness of who I was on the inside. All of the hurt. All of the pain. All of the hateful things I did and said about myself. All of the shame I carried from shit that I'd done.

I turned my back to the mirror and slid down onto the floor of my bathroom. I wept like a newborn baby who had just come into the world and into everything unfamiliar. Lying on that floor, I knew I had to accept who I was, what I had done, and who I had allowed to come into my life and wreck me to pieces. If I hadn't done that, I would never have been able to fully face my truth.

As my sister-friend reminded me in Dallas, "The Time Is Now." Words that I would come to live by.

My process began.

The Naked Truth

You see I had finally realized the things I accepted, the men I chose and the behavior I had been displaying was all a part of the layered pain I had experienced but had not stopped to deal with it. I was living a life fully wounded in heart and mind from my past hurt. I no longer wanted to live a lie. I no longer wanted to be a fake to this world or better yet to myself. I know in order to deal with my past I had to call out the things about myself that I knew to be wrong, in order to change something it must be acknowledged. I found this to be the first time I really felt guidance from God by way of me truly accepting and creating an intimate relationship with the Most High about what love really is. I knew it was time for me to love the real me, the me that had been scared to show up in fear of having to be alone. I quickly understood when you know and love your true self and you understand that it is okay to show up in this world without a mask that then you really get to live freely. I was so grateful for my encounter in the midnight with my God and Thankful that my time had arrived to come out from the dark and show the world my real light. Freeing myself from the lies and the fake relationships and friends was like a new gasping of fresh air that new life needs to make. I understood Fear to mean to me as Face Everything And Recover and I had decided I would no longer accept anything that was a lie and I begin to tell truths to myself daily and that the quicker I could do that the quicker I could recover and not have to hold on to pain and blossom into to woman I knew was deep down inside of me. I decided to make the famous saying, "I am the master of my fate, I am the captain of my soul, along with God's grace and my being completely naked and truthful with myself the things that would fuel the woman I was destined to become, the woman I desired to be. I was so glad I was choosing me and not the pain of my past anymore.

I will instruct you and teach you in the way you should go; I will counsel you with my loving eye on you.
Psalm 32:8 (NIV)

9
DESIRES OF MY HEART

You see, here is the thing! As I sat there in that house preparing to move into my new apartment, I felt an overwhelming presence of self-awareness and I began to think. A lot. There is something about getting ready to move that makes you reflect on the chapter of your life that you are about to close.

Since that visit to Texas and everything that had happened since, God had been giving me so much clarity. I could not shake the feeling that all of this was a new start for me, the start of something amazing. I need to begin again. New Nicole. New life.

Although I was not physically bound to this place, there was something here that was holding me captive. I was being held to a love and a man that would never be mine. I was held to debt that I could never repay. I was held to a woman who was broken in so many places that she would never be whole. At least not here.

My biggest revelation as I packed those boxes was that God saw and knew it all. There was nothing that happened with me or to me that He was not aware of. I started to understand and believe there were things that were allowed to happen to me, like this relationship, because, somehow, it was going to bless me. Just like all of the other trials in my life. But unlike times before, I had to do something first before God could move me to where He wanted me to go. Before, I felt like His grace and protection carried me through life like a baby, one who was naïve and oblivious to the arms that lifted, fed, and kept me from harm. But now, as a good and grown woman, I could no longer use youth as an excuse. God had brought me front and center in my life, forcing me to stare myself and my shit in the eye. There was no denying it now. No turning back. I needed to get TRUTHFULLY NAKED with myself about who I was, what I'd done, how I've behaved, what I've hidden from for so long.

It was time for me to be stripped of all the things that made me feel secure. All of the material things that meant nothing and the false sense of love and security that I got from the men in my life in exchange for my loyalty and body. To get my breakthrough, I had to be broken. Broken free from all of the stuff and people and acceptance and even the beauty that I thought I needed. I would have to go through a process, and while I didn't know every step I would have to take, I knew what was required of me. Brutal honesty. With myself and everyone around me.

I'd been crying out, knowing that I was living wrong in so many ways, but asking for God's help, only to turn right back around and continue doing things my way. Don't get me wrong now, I still believed in God's goodness for my life. I never believed that God had abandoned me. I knew better. But let's be clear about something. Knowing and understanding the power of God are two different things. I understood. But I didn't know.

To begin to know, I had to come to grips with the fact that my choices were mine, not my circumstances. I created the chaos in my life. That was not the men and it certainly was not God. God wanted more for me. He had more for me. I just needed to want it for myself.

I'd finally come to a cross road as I had many times before. I had to make a decision about what was next for my life. This time, it felt like life or death. I had to choose what to believe and what path to follow. Either I was going to go God's way or my way. If I followed Him, everything was completely out of my control, and I wasn't used to that—at all. I had been putting God on the back burner, picking and choosing the parts of Him that I liked at times, but remaining in the driver's seat of my own life. If I followed Him, I would have to surrender my license and become a passenger. A quiet, willing one at that. I knew the dangerous, curvy road that I would have to drive alone if I turned my back on Him this time. And the thought of that terrified me.

I sat on the floor, surrounded by boxes and bubble wrap, and got real. I flat-out asked myself, "Nicole, will you trust and believe God's promise to you, or will you continue to do what is easiest?"

I decided I wanted everything that was mine. I wanted all that God promised for my life and with wanting that, it meant that I would have to walk into the dark of the unknown. I would have to wander into this unchartered territory, these deep, deep waters, and trust that God wouldn't let me drown. I would have to close my eyes, take His hand, and listen to his direction. I could never stop or let go until I KNEW His promise and no longer just understand it.

I accepted that the time had come to break free of all things not of God in my life. There was still one last piece that I was holding onto. I didn't know why, but I knew when God says clear everything that stands between you and Him, He means everything. I hadn't planned for it to unfold the way it did, nor was I prepared! Something in my spirit said that when I made this call, it would unravel so much in my life and that what I thought would be an outcome I could control would turn out otherwise.

I said a simple, but intimate, prayer for my future, and I made up in my mind that I was ready for what was for me.

"In Jesus Name," I said and picked up the phone.

"Hey, where are you?" I said with such a condescending tone when Mr. Can't Get Right answered. "Are you still in Chicago with your daughter? I thought you were going to bring me the money."

When he got quiet, I figured what was next. Here come the lies in five, four, three, two, and one…

> "Nicole, I'm sorry. This is what happened. My daughter had to go to the hospital. She fractured her ankle and I had to stay here with her."

> "You promised me I could count on you. I don't have any other way to get it."

> "I'm sorry, but I won't be back for a few days 'cause I still have to unpack her stuff and set up her dorm room."

> "Yeah, okay. Fine," I said.

I was counting on that money to help me move. When I asked him weeks ago, he assured me that he'd have it. I knew better than to believe that. But that was the last little bit of belief in him that I was holding on to. The last piece of an old life and an old me. Still I was emotional about facing what was right in front of me.

We hung up the phone and I called a friend to explain the bind I was in.

After listening to me go off, she asked, "Why you sound so pissed? It's not his fault," referring to what happened with his daughter.

"'Cause I don't believe him, girl. You know he lie so damn much."

"Come on now, Nicole. I don't think he would lie about his daughter being hurt. That's a bit much, don't you think?"

I couldn't imagine a parent lying on their child like that. "Well, yeah, I guess you're right. I'm just tripping 'cause I don't know what to do. It's cool though. I'm about to go to bed. Let me call you back tomorrow."

I woke up the next day and text him. After talking with my girl the night before, I felt guilty about being mad with him and being selfish when he was really dealing with something serious. I just wanted to know how his daughter was. He didn't bother to respond to any of my messages. I gave up.

I got dressed and decided to go see my friend at her barbershop. I sat and chatted it up with her for a while, as we talked, I got this strong urge to go to the shop where Can't Get Right cut hair. I said a quick goodbye to her, hopped in my car, and headed his way.

As I was stopped at a red light just one block up from his shop, I looked over at the parking lot next to the building. I could have sworn I saw his truck parked there. But as far as I knew, he was still out of town. Something definitely wasn't right.

I quickly pulled my car over to a side street and attempted to call him again. And what do you know, this time, he answers.

"Hey baby! What's up with you?" He seems a little too amped to me. But it could have just been that my antennas were up.

"Oh, nothing," I said nonchalantly. "I text you earlier several times and you didn't respond."

"Oh, yeah I was moving my daughter's stuff to the dorm room. They have her on crutches too so I had to help her up all the steps of the building. I'm super tired."

"What does that have to do with you answering your phone just to tell me that?"

"Listen, baby, my phone was in the truck and the battery went dead. With me doing all this stuff I didn't put it on the charger."

"Oh really?"

"Yes, baby."

"Okay, then so are you back in St. Louis?"

"Nawl, I'm still out of town in Chicago."

"Well let me know when you get back."

"As soon as I get back, I will call you baby."

"Alright," I said as I hung up the phone with a bird's eye view of his truck just a block over from where I was parked.

"Oh, he's still in Chicago huh? Oh, okay," I said aloud as I put my car in drive to head on over to his barbershop. As I am walking up to the door, one of the other barbers who works there sees me.

"Hey lady! How are you?" He is loud as usual as he open the door for me.

"Oh, I'm awesome. Thanks for asking." I proceed inside. I scan the shop for Can't Get Right, but I don't see him.

"Hey where yo' boy at?" I asked the barber who had the chair next to his.

"He's in the bathroom back there." He motioned with his head towards the rear of the shop.

"Ohhh, okay. Cool." I took a seat in the waiting area.

It seemed like forever for him to come out of the bathroom only because I was sitting there pissed off. I couldn't believe all of this unnecessary lying. I sat there, boiling, and I heard the bathroom door open. Here he comes walking out just as normal as ever, with a white paper towel, drying his hands. His head was down, but just like in a movie, he slowly looked up on his way back to his chair to throw the paper towel away. That's when he saw me sitting there and our eyes locked.

You would have thought he saw the resurrection of a deceased loved one. I mean, it was like the life was sucked from his body, the moment his eyes landed on my face.

I sat there with a genuine smile on my face. His reaction was quite comical actually.

He took a second to gather his thoughts as he came over to me. "Hey baby!"

I kept smiling and kept it cool. "Hey to you. Can I have a lining? I just need you to clean up my neck line."

He was so shook he didn't know what to do. I got up, sat in his chair, and didn't say a word. He grabbed his clippers and proceeded to shape up the nape of my neck. I wore my hair pulled up often for work because my locs were so long so this was a must at least once every two weeks to.

> "Just so you know, I just got back here baby," he said out of nowhere.
>
> "Oh is that right?"
>
> "Yes, I swear to you."
>
> "Okay, that's fine, if that's what you say."

He wiped my neckline with a Sanek neck strip and astringent.

"So you're not mad baby?"

I didn't respond. I got up and headed to the door. He followed me out and walked beside me to my car. I turned to face him.

"Hey, it is what it is. No I'm not mad and I'm not doing this with you and your lies anymore."

"Oh, you not doing this with me anymore? What is that supposed to mean, Nicole?"

"It means I want more than the lies you give. I've dealt with lies before from a husband and I'm just no longer willing to accept them from anybody else. So it's been nice but it's over for me." I tried to get in my car, but he grabbed my arm, stopping me.

"What if I'm not done?"

"Well I don't know what to tell you because a relationship with me is dead in the water." I snatched my arm away and started up my car.

He wedged himself in the door, refusing to move, and held on to the handle on the inside so I couldn't close it. He gave me a glaring stare for a moment. "So that's it, huh? I guess I didn't mean shit to you, huh Nicole?"

"Look nothing you say will matter to me at this point. We have come to that place where we must move on and that's it, so please move out of my doorway so I can leave."

I stared him right in his eyes. He knew it was over.

"Yeah alright, Nicole. Well I'll let you go, but just so you know after I finish at the shop tonight I was bringing you that money like I said I would. But I guess since we are over, there is no need for that, huh?"

Taking hold of the handle on my car door, I looked up with a smile on my face. "You are correct, there is no need for that," I said confidently. I closed my door and drove away, watching him in my rear view mirror still standing in the place I left him as he got smaller the further I drove away.

I felt the light again. I was overjoyed about what was to come for me, and I drove home to finish packing and to continue to get mentally prepared for the move I was about to embark upon. It was all coming together. Out with my old and in with my new.

Once I got into my new place and many months later, I was lying down one night and it hit me that for first time in my life, I was in bed alone. It was the first time since I was thirteen years old and I did not have a boyfriend or some guy I could call to entertain me, even if I wasn't really interested in dating him. So much had changed.

I also noticed that Mr. Railroad had become more and more of a stranger to me. His calls and texts became further and further apart and his visits had pretty much stopped altogether even before my move. I never saw him anymore, at least in my personal space that's for sure. If I was out with my friends I would run into him from time to time. He would pull me aside to talk to me and blow me a lot of smoke, meaning funky conversation that wasn't about much and full of promises that he'd never keep. It didn't matter if I never heard from him again since I had already decided that sexy little fling I had with him was surely over for me. You can't be with someone and you never see or spend time with them. Since my last serious conversation with Mr. Railroad, I made it perfectly clear on where I stood and how it was going to be if things didn't change. His actions told me everything I needed to know. I was done.

Now this meant, yo' girl, yes little ol' me, was in a total sex drought for the first time in, oh my gosh I can't even tell you when. Let me be honest, I NEVER had a problem with having that go-to sex partner somewhere in the background before and after my marriage. The periods I went without a man physically were brief. But satisfying my physical needs was detrimental to my spirit. I needed to step out of that mess to see it.

Six months later, I was feeling like a new woman. Sex was a release, but the drama that came with it cluttered my mind. Celibacy took yo' girl to new levels! I could just sit with myself and get really focused on understanding of who and what I really wanted. It felt so, so good.

I started to enjoy my new way of life and the ease of it all compared to the chaos circle I was in when I was dating. The days continued to pass and my life became calmer and more in tune with where I wanted to be spiritually. I found myself going to church service a little more regularly. I was taking personal time to meditate and keep my head and heart aligned with what I said I wanted. I was beginning to enjoy the company of my good girlfriends and really radiating from the inside out, not just a half-hearted smile that I usually wore when I wasn't really happy. I was actually smiling from my heart.

I started to learn me and take a hard look at what I had gone through. I was working through those emotions and understanding how and where I went wrong in some of the decisions I had made in my past and why I made those choices. I let go of all of the ill feeling towards anyone who may have been involved in a particular painful time from my past, including my parents, my daughter's father, my ex-husband, and all of the men I'd dealt with. This was my pain, my choices, my life. I owned it. I saw it.

Spending some time with myself with no mask was a much needed journey I never even knew I needed to take.

Before I knew it, it was a brand new year. My resolution was, "I was going to enjoy being single, love on my girls and myself, and take one day at time." I meant every word. I wanted joy in my life. I wanted to take the time to savor all this new, good stuff that was coming into my life. I just wanted to breathe.

As the new year rolled in, I decided to change my social media name from "Nikki Rob" to "Nicole 'I Deserve It All'" because I realized I really did deserve it all. I should have all that my heart desired. I wouldn't settle ever again. Not in any way.

I'd been searching for yet another place to move before the holidays, and I finally found it. I was soon packing for the third time in six months but only into a longer unit within my current apartment complex. I did happily. I was willing to follow God and my peace of mind to the end of the earth. Wherever I needed to go, I would go.

Valentine's Day was approaching, and it came and went with a blur. How things had changed from my past, huh? Unlike the fiasco before, my heart was so happy. I kept right on going, packing and purging more of my old life. I decided that with this move, I would get rid of absolutely everything that reminded me of those relationships I played around with and that had me living a selfish lie with myself and wearing a mask! I sold my bedroom set and mattresses, gave away bedding and bath towel sets. I threw away lingerie, shredded pictures, and threw out memorable items that no longer served me anymore from those relationships.

I took a three-day break from work to finish clearing all of those old things out and to get organized. On my last night, I spent that evening talking to my friend in Dallas and binge watching Lifetime movies. After I hung up with her, I found myself perusing social media. I had a notification that someone had commented on an old photo. So I open it and saw an old image from about two years ago that I'd posted. I'd taken the picture at a conference in Kansas City where I was a vendor selling my sterling silver jewelry. I scrolled down to the new comment.

"Turn around and let me see the back of your hair!" The comment was from someone named "Zulu Love." That was his alias for social media, of course. I knew him and we'd flirted back and forth for years.

I fell out laughing. "One of these days." I responded to him. In a good mood, I decided to send him a private message.

"You better stop coming for me out in public like that!"

He quickly responded. "What, would you rather me say, Turn around and let me see yo' ass?"

I laughed again. After a few more messages, I wrote, "Hey do you wanna take me on a date?"

"Yeah right, are you serious? 'Cause you have a PhD in playing games. You been playing with me for a minute now."

"Yes, I'm serious. Do you have a woman? And don't lie!"

He was on it. "I ain't gon' lie, and no I don't have woman. Just so you know, I don't date Police Officers, but for you, I'll make an exception."

"LMAO!" I wrote back. "Oh you will, huh?"

"Sure, if you are serious."

"I am."

"Are you off tonight?"

"Yep. I go back tomorrow."

"Damn I wished you had jumped in my inbox before now. You could have gone to this jazz event with me."

"Oh, I can go." I was excited about the idea of seeing him and going out.

"It's too late now. I asked my father to go with me."

He asked for my number and shared that he'd be available on Sunday if I would be too. I was, so we made plans to confirm a place and time that day.

"Oh, and, before I let you go, Happy Belated Birthday to you," I wrote before he logged off.

(Big Ups to social media! They help people to remember friends special days!)☺

Well, alrighty then! I thought. Hopefully he thought it was nice of me to say something about his birthday. I shut down my scrolling for the night and smiled as I drifted off to sleep.

Sunday came and the date was a success, so much so that we shut the restaurant down. We had such great conversation that we lost track of time and they practically had to put us out of the place. As we got ready to leave, it was clear that neither of us were quite ready for the night to end. Walking back to my car, I had an idea.

> "Hey, I want to show you something. It's an art sculpture I think you will appreciate. It's super dope. Follow me."

We hop in our cars and I drove a short distance around the corner. We pull up and get out.

As we approach the huge statue, his mouth dropped. "What the hell! WOW, what is it?"

> "It's a steel man coming out of the ground and the artist calls it 'The Awakening'! It's dope, ain't it?"

> "Yeah, that's pretty interesting."

As he stood staring at the sculpture, I stood staring at him, in amazement, thinking about how we originally met. I was this man's bank teller twenty years ago and now we'd known each other for twenty years and have worked at the same job for the last fourteen years. In that time. I got married, had a second child, and got divorced. He'd been married, had more kids, and was divorced too. Now here we were, after all that flirting between marriages over the years, and wrapping up a great first date. I felt like an excited teenager who had just passed the driver's test. I was ecstatic about the friendship that was to come. Glancing at the sculpture and then placing my eyes back on him, and trying to let him catch me staring, I felt tingly all over. Could God be giving me a second chance! At love, at life, at everything. I just felt really good that night.

I could, and still can, barely explain the level of gratitude and grace I feel I've been given. I feel when we make a conscious decision about who we really are and what we really want, and we began to walk in that thing with our whole selves, God will grant us the desires of our heart.

Even though I started exploring the possibilities and allowing myself to love again after being single for quite sometime now, I was approaching it so much differently this time. I knew exactly how I wanted to feel. I wanted a relationship that mirrored the one that I now had with myself. I no longer wanted sadness and half happy days. I wanted to wake up with an amazing happiness that I created for me, not by a man. I wanted to like and love myself before the man that should be in my life would show himself.

It was mind-blowing to me how my season of sexual abstinence, self-awareness, and often loneliness had completely shifted everything for me. I spent so much of my life focused on what I needed to be for a man to love me, and not nearly enough on what I needed to love myself. I didn't know it then but I know it now—and I am never going back.

I am never going back to my past. I am never going back to the woman I was, the one who was loved for what she was on the outside and not for her inner beauty. I was never going back to the lies. I was never going back to a heart and spirit that I held in my hands, in pieces.

I was whole now. A whole woman with a whole heart. And I was ready to give and to receive love with it.

The Naked Truth

When you allow God to come into your life and give Him all of you, as He asks, transformation takes place.

Making changes to what you are used to is no easy task but we must understand, if we want something different we must be willing and accepting to do something different. If we halfway change, we get half of what we want. When you are ready for new things to come into your life. When you are tired of faking the smiles by wearing the mask and you are tired of being something you no longer desire for yourself, change is the key. There is no way around it and you can't cheat it. I wanted everything that was mine and for me to have it, it required me to give up everything that was familiar and I had to do it freely. But you see the gift of peace and love for yourself that would be giving in return would be worth more than this life could give.

Trust in the Lord with all your heart, And lean not on your own understanding; In all your ways acknowledge Him, And He shall direct your paths.

Proverbs 3:5-6 (NKJV)

10

TRUTH MY NEW BEST FRIEND

A s you each hold your separate containers of sand, they represent your lives to this moment; individual and unique. As you now combine your sand together, your lives also join as one.

Now as these grains of sand can never be separated, our prayer for you today is that your lives together will be longer than the time it would take to separate the individual grains of sand."

I was standing at the altar, looking in my soon-to-be husband's eyes, with my daughters and the boys who shortly, would officially become my sons. The pastor spoke final words over us before pronouncing us husband and wife. We were indeed becoming one.

I was glowing like a ray of sunshine in my beautiful, satin wedding gown adorned with pearls and lace, and a crystal bezel tiara. Had you told me, two years ago, that I would be here, pledging my life and love to a man I've known for over twenty years, I wouldn't have believed you. I could never have imagined that I would be a wife again. That I would have this man. That he would truly be my happily ever after. Every possible emotion flowed through me. Happiness. Amazement. Gratefulness for God's grace.

> "I now pronounce you husband and wife. Kevin, you may kiss your bride."

To hear the word "bride" again brought me to tears. This time, it meant something different to me. This was my second chance at love. This was my second chance to get it right, to love this man fully and completely, free from pain and disappointment and on a solid foundation of truth, trust, love, friendship, and respect. I could give him all of that, just as he could give all of that to me.

As night fell and our wedding day came to a close, we said our goodbyes to our family and friends and started on this road as husband and wife. The beginning of our life together was nothing short of blessed. I truly began to understand that God is faithful and you can take Him at His word. Our new life was a beautiful testament to that.

For starters, my husband bought me the house of my dreams. Do you remember my oldest daughter, the one who I bought into this world when I was sixteen? She graduated from college! You can imagine how I shouted and gave God an ugly praise and a face full of tears on that day, right in the corner of the civic center after the commencement ceremony. And on top of that, a few months later, my husband got a promotion on his job. This all happened within a period of 14 months. Blessings on top of blessings.

Speaking of blessings, let me be clear and transparent. I don't want you to be fooled into thinking that God gives you any of this without a test. So let me tell you about everything that happened in between all of those wonderful things in our life, that made us that much more grateful for each and every one of them...

Three months after my wedding, I started having severe pain in my leg. Severe was an understatement—it was unbearable. I was forced to stop working only to find out that I needed major hip surgery. While my doctor urged me to go under the knife right away, he also explained that I'd be in recovery for several weeks afterwards, which meant I would be unable to travel for my daughter's college graduation. I knew immediately that was not an option for me. There was nothing, I mean nothing, that could have kept me from that ceremony. So I opted for high doses of pain medication to get me through.

When I went in for surgery after we returned home, what should have been an outpatient procedure became a three-day hospital stay due to complications and extreme pain that my doctor hadn't anticipated. I came back to the new, two-story home that we'd been blessed with, but couldn't walk up the stairs to my beautiful bedroom.

We'd barely unpacked, yet I was confined to the couch. I couldn't work for five months. The physical therapy to learn to walk again was grueling, some of the hardest physical work that I'd ever done. As I sat on my sofa, unable to move day in and day out, it wasn't long before my spirit sank deeper and deeper. I'd been blessed to marry a man designed specifically for my heart, and couldn't serve him as a wife for what would end up being ten months due to unending pain. I couldn't unpack my house to make it a home. By this time I was on unpaid leave and extended medical coverage, yet

my husband being who he is, kicked it up a notch to keep us covered and so our home wouldn't miss my income. He worked double, triple time, to cover his house, all with two bulging discs in his back that could give him major issues and prevent him from moving or working at any given time. Thank God that didn't happen. He took such good care of me while working as hard as he did. I couldn't have asked for a better partner in my life.

Even with the love and support I had, it wasn't long before I spiraled into all-time emotional low. Being dependent, in every way, was devastating for me. I was never a woman who did not contribute to her own household and take care of her family. My spirit was as broken as my hip. I felt useless and afraid. I started to lose hope.

I knew I had so much to be grateful for. Yet my prayers always began with gratefulness, but ended with pleas to God to tell me why. Why was this happening to me now? Just when my life became brighter and I had so much to look forward to and be happy for. I had a brand new husband, home, a business I was trying to build and a host of responsibilities that only I could handle, but I was unable to because I was literally handicapped and could not get around without help. It became clear that God was sitting me down. I just didn't understand why.

But I kept praying for God's help. I stayed in constant fellowship with my journey sister in Texas, and she held me up spiritually during those times that I wanted to fall flat.

You may be thinking, okay, so what does that have to do with anything, Nicole? You were talking to me about love and life, and how you finally found the love of your life, despite some challenges.

Well, I'll tell you.

For me, this season was another opportunity to see how, even in my distress, I must learn to wait on and trust God's plan for my life every step of the way— not just on my good days but also on my bad days. When I decided to become a mother at sixteen, all of the odds of life began to stack against me. Homelessness. Helplessness. Depression. Suicide attempt. Fighting to be able to walk with my graduating high school class. Emotional abuse, infidelity, adultery, divorce, and more heartbreaks that I can count. But in each of those seasons, no matter how low I thought I was, God was always there to carry me. His favor was always the reward for my faith. Whenever I grew weary from my struggles, accepted when I'd done all I could do, and gave the rest to Him, He sent someone or something to remind me that I still had everything to live for. All I had to do was hold on.

At each twist and turn in my life I found myself in a holding pattern. Actually, it was more of a resting place. While healing from my surgery, for the first time in a long time, I was reminded of how whenever I found myself up against a wall in my life, God held me in that place before the storm completely took over. I realized that God had been using those experiences to prepare me for my life's purpose. Each defining situation in my life was to grow and stretch me to be what He has called me to be. And He would always bring me through.

The physical pain and recovery from a major surgery could have broken me. (But it didn't. I am healthy and whole.) The emotional pain, heartbreak and brokenness I experienced in my first marriage, by most people's account, should have taken me out of the dating game completely, let alone the second-time bride game. The men in between should have taken every ounce of pride and belief in love I had before I could even get to the husband I have now. That didn't happen. I grew stronger. I grew better. I learned.

Through each heartbreak, each test, my lessons always brought me back to me. I had to learn about love of myself and others, respect, and honesty, the foundation of any relationship that God designs. Loving myself was so key. If I had known who I was or what my worth was, I would not have been in any of those relationships that dishonored me. To discover that worth, I had to tell the truth.

When I finally allowed myself to tell the truth about who I really was, what I had been doing, who I had been attracting and the life I was living. I would still be broken, living a lie, feeling unworthy, accepting chaos and wicked, unhealthy soul ties. But God kept coming for me until I could see and accept it all as my truth.

The day I accepted all of me, who I was, was the day I got to make the decision to become who I was called to be. A woman worthy of self-love, even with a past like mine. A woman who deserves love from a man who is mine and mine alone. A woman who can speak freely about my mistakes but not let my mistakes speak for me or rule who I am. A woman free from pain, although she's had her heart shattered in a million pieces a million times. She is free of her insecurities, trust issues, and doubt.

That woman is me.

Finally, I've accepted my truth, and that allowed me to heal all sides of my heart and negative mental spaces that housed the memories of heartbreak, disappointment, and frustration. I can now say that while I may have lost myself in the past and the tangled and deceptive life I lived before God met me in my dreams one night, today, I am the woman who lives a life of peace, love, and gratefulness. I am a believer in second chances.

I am standing fully, boldly, and bravely in my Naked Truth.

And I am holding out my hand to you, praying that you can join me and do the same.

"I have no greater joy than to hear that my children are walking in the TRUTH."

3 John 1:4 (NIV)